195

STEEL SHIP "TROOP"
STRANDED ON LONG ISLAND COAST
NEAR FORGE RIVER LIFE S.S. STATION

MAY 24 TH 1898

The St. John, New Brunswick iron ship *Troop* came ashore in fog on the Great South Beach of Long Island near Moriches Inlet on May 24, 1898. The Life Savers from the Forge River station rigged the breeches buoy, but the crew would not come ashore because sea conditions were calm. Wreckers refloated the vessel eleven days later and took her to New York City. *Photo from the collection of Capt. W.J.L. Parker, U.S.C.G.* [*Ret.*]

SHIPWRECKS
AROUND NEW ENGLAND

(Illustrated)

By William P. Quinn

A chronology of marine accidents and
disasters from Grand Manan to Sandy Hook

The *Kenwood* came ashore on Cedar Point, Scituate, Massachusetts during a gale on February 4, 1926. She was bound from Halifax to Boston with lumber and was a total loss. The crew was rescued by the Coast Guard. *Photo courtesy of the U.S. Coast Guard, Washington, D.C.*

COPYRIGHT, ©, 1979, BY WILLIAM P. QUINN

All rights reserved

Library of Congress Catalog Card No. 79-88076

ISBN-0-936972-05-X

Printed in the United States of America

Published by
The Lower Cape Publishing Co.
P.O. Box 901, Orleans, Masachusetts 02653

FIRST EDITION (Third Printing)

PREFACE

Shipwrecks around New England are dramatic events. Historically they number in the thousands, from the rocky coast of Maine, down past the Capes of Massachusetts, and through the Sounds past Long Island to Sandy Hook, New Jersey. This seaboard is one of the most active maritime areas in the world. Shipwrecks sometimes cause death, injury and loss of property. Davy Jones' locker is full of valuable prizes for salvors able to retrieve them. This book is a collection of photographs of marine accidents and disasters. The coverage extends south and west of New England to include Long Island, New York and the Hudson River, and north to Nova Scotia. Each chapter reviews a decade beginning in the 1870's. It is perhaps significant that, at that time, advancements in the field of photography coincided with the establishment of the United States Life Saving Service. The two are dominant features of this book.

Not all of the shipwrecks around New England are listed. The number is far too great for the space. The theme is aimed at graphic illustrations designed to take the reader to the scene and witness the wreck. The written text will summarize some of the maritime news and important disasters along with some of the pertinent history of the decade. The material was largely gleaned from the newspapers of the era. In the early days, one of the worst habits of the mariner was spinning yarns. The sailor was usually the only survivor reporting the details surrounding a marine accident. The information obviously had to be verified from many other sources. Personal contact with some of the old sea captains still alive provides a link with the past, but few of them are left. The various marine publications and periodicals, and Government publications, round out the main source of material.

For the past 100 years, travel by passenger steamer in New England coastal waters has, at various times, been risky. Progress, modern technology and higher safety standards have reduced the risks. The higher costs of modernization have eliminated most of the steamers. The Coast Guard, while maintaining its readiness for "search and rescue" are also in pursuit of the modern drug smuggler, and have to enforce new laws against pollution in the waterways. The picturesque days of commercial sailing vessels are gone. Somehow, the old traditions and romance of the sea are still there, but most of the nostalgia is found in the marine museums.

This book is dedicated with love to my wife

MARY

for her many hours of help and assistance
in the completion of this book.

For the shipwreck buff, this would seem to be a bonanza. It is, however, a Staten Island graveyard for tugs, barges, ferries and excursion boats. There are several derelict marine craft at the Witte Marine Salvage yard on Arthur Kill. Many of the vessels are lying atop other broken hulls, rotting away in the mud. *Aerial Photography by William P. Quinn.*

CONTENTS

LIST OF PHOTOGRAPHS

Above: The Nova Scotia barkentine *Persia* stranded on Long Beach, New York, on March 16, 1902. The weather was thick, with a strong southeast wind. Life Savers landed the crew of ten with the breeches buoy. The vessel suffered damage to her rigging, and the hull had a pronounced hog. Wreckers floated the vessel ten days later. The ship was of 598 tons, bound from Buenos Aires to New York with a cargo of hides. *Photo from the collection of Paul C. Morris, Nantucket, Mass.* **Below:** On March 14, 1916, a serious fire aboard the *S. S. Herman Winter* caused her to be towed out of Portland, Maine, harbor to the south shore and beached. Fire boats pumped so much water into the after hold that she sank and rested on the soft bottom mud. Wreckers removed much of her damaged cargo and refloated her on March 26th. She was then towed to Boston and was repaired in a drydock. *Photo courtesy of the Mariners Museum, Newport News, Virginia.*

CHAPTER ONE

As long as men have sailed ships on the sea, a shipwreck on shore has had a fascinating appeal for people to rush to the scene to view the disaster and to witness the rescue effort to save the crew. The first maritime accident in New England was probably never entered in the record books. It may have been one of the early Norse explorers stranded on the shoals near Nantucket, Massachusetts, or driven by a storm onto the rocky coasts of Maine or Rhode Island, or possibly further south on Long Island, New York. Since the mid 1600's the annals show that thousands of vessels have been wrecked on the New England coastline from Eastport, Maine to Sandy Hook, New Jersey. Numerous accidents have also occurred on the Hudson and St. Lawrence rivers. Early town records relate vivid accounts of suffering and death along the shores. The principal cause was the capricious New England weather. This coastline is among the busiest maritime commerce areas in the world. In the past 100 years the ships navigating New England waters have met with various and sometimes tragic mishaps.

Countless ships have been sunk or capsized in storms, while numerous others have been stranded on beaches. There were collisions - ships striking ships - with one or both sunk as a result, ships hitting bridges; ships running up on partially sunken derelicts; or even ramming whales. Icebergs took their toll in the dense fogs of the North Atlantic. Accidents were caused by boiler explosions or fires, and sometimes were the result of arson. Propulsion equipment would break down at the wrong time. Schooners would lose their sails in a gale. Disasters occurred because of a lost rudder, or structural failure of the hull. There were war losses by torpedoes or mines and even scuttling. The list seems endless. Human error was a major factor in many mishaps. There was failure of crewmen because of illness, injury, exhaustion, drunkenness, sabotage or mutiny. There were many cases of a ship setting sail and never being heard from again. There were mysterious events like the New York brigantine *Mary Celeste,* found under full sail in the mid Atlantic in December of 1872 with no trace of the crew. There were other causes. Mooncussers, those unsavory wreckers, lured ships ashore on dark nights with false lights.

The rescue of shipwrecked mariners was carried out, albeit rather poorly, for many years prior to the 1850's by volunteers of the Massachusetts Humane Society which was formed in 1786 for the relief of the sailor cast ashore. The society built small sheds along the shores and furnished them with canned foods, first aid kits, a fireplace with fuel, and flares. They called them charity houses. The Commonwealth of Massachusetts and the Federal Government made contributions to the Society to help defray the costs of the houses along the coasts. The only other aid for the distressed mariner was the wrecker on his daily trek down the beach.

Congress recognized this problem and began to move toward relief for the distressed seaman. In 1848, in a moving speech, Congressman William A. Newell of New Jersey opened the fight for the establishment of a Life Saving Service. In an effort to convince Congress of the need for more protection along the nation's shorelines he vividly described the horrible scenes of a shipwreck which he had witnessed along the shores of his home state. Congress became convinced, and a small appropriation was voted. Funds were made available to purchase surfboats and other life saving devices, but all of this depended upon volunteers to man the equipment.

In the winter of 1870-71 several disasters occurred on the coasts with heavy loss of life. It was clear that more had to be done, and Congress at that time voted to appropriate $200,000 to reorganize the service, dismiss inefficient personnel, hire new men and buy better equipment to

Publications prior to the development of photography used lithographs to illustrate marine disasters. **Above:** The steamer *Lexington* caught fire in Long Island Sound on the night of January 13, 1840. Captain George Child with a crew of forty, tried desperately to head the vessel toward shore. There were 150 passengers on board, and a full cargo of bales of cotton, which fed the flames. The fire burned out of control, and the ship sank. There were only four survivors. **Below:** The bark *Vernon* ashore on Lynn beach on February 3, 1859. Men on the shore launched boats into the rough seas to save those aboard the grounded vessel. *Photo reproductions courtesy of the Peabody Museum of Salem.*

protect the lives and property along the coasts. New stations were built. Modern innovations in lifesaving were introduced, and the death toll was reduced. Men experienced in boat handling and the sea were hired to row the lifeboats and to shoot lines to wrecked vessels to bring the survivors to shore on the breeches buoy. They walked the lonely shorelines on the beach patrols and with flares warned ships that ventured too close to shore. They ulitmately manned 283 Life Saving Stations along the east and west coasts and the Great Lakes of the United States. Several of these intrepid men became heroes, and many died trying to save others. Some years later, motor lifeboats relieved the men of the back-breaking strain of rowing for miles, fighting mountainous waves.

The modern term is "Beachcomber," but in the early days because of the numerous wrecks he was called a "Wrecker." It was generally agreed that the flotsam and jetsam washed up on the beaches after a wreck was the property of the one who found it. Some days were better than others and the wreckers managed to eke out a living from the sea. After a shipwreck when the salvaged goods were sold, all that remained was the hull, which was cut up for firewood to keep their homes warm in the winter. There was usually plenty of debris on the beach to keep the home fires burning even during the coldest winters. There were many wreckers along the shores, and at times there was violence at the scene of a wreck. On March 4, 1875, an intense northeast storm drove the Italian bark *Giovanni* ashore at Peaked Hill Bars in Provincetown, Massachusetts. Fourteen men were lost in the mountainous seas and the vessel broke up on the outer bar. As the bodies washed ashore the wreckers battled each other over the gold rings and watches from the dead sailors. There was mayhem and attempted murder among the men on the beach.

The annual reports of the United States Life Saving Service were published by the Government from 1876 through 1914. They relate vivid accounts of daring rescues, unselfish devotion to duty and exemplary performances of honorable men so that in the forty years, from the commencement of the service until it was merged with the Revenue Cutter Service on January 28, 1915 to form the United States Coast Guard, there were numerous first class gold medals awarded for service above and beyond the call of duty. The Life Savers did succeed in putting the Mooncusser out of business permanently. In the first few years of operations the Life Saving Service rescued thousands of shipwrecked persons and saved millions in property.

The Life Saving Service report for the year 1889 records the wreck of the schooner *Oliver Dyer* and the heroic efforts of the crew of the Jerrys Point L.S. station on the coast of New Hampshire on the morning of November 26, 1888. The schooner was out of Weehawken, New Jersey, for Saco, Maine with a cargo of coal and a crew of five. The vessel was anchored just inside the entrance to Portsmouth harbor to wait out the heavy weather. The gale, however, caused the schooner to part her anchor chains and to be cast upon the rock ledges about fifty yards from shore. When the craft struck the ledges the sea washed over her and filled the hull driving the crew into the fore and main rigging. One man was washed overboard and lost. Two others seeing the Life Savers on the beach leaped into the raging waters and were hauled out by the surfmen near shore. Two other men were in the rigging of the schooner. The Life Savers waded out onto a rock ledge and heaved a line to these men. They were hauled ashore by the surfmen who themselves were in danger of being caught in the heavy seas and dangerous undertow while perched precariously on the rocks. More than once they had to save one another while carrying out the rescue of the crew of the schooner. The weather was very cold and stormy. The Life Savers found themselves in the water pulling out the survivors at the risk of their own lives. For the daring rescue of the four crewmen, gold lifesaving medals were awarded to Keeper Silas H. Harding and the six surfmen: George W. Randall, Winslow A. Amazeen, Ephraim S. Hall, Selden F. Wells, Ernest Robinson and John Smith. The ship was a total loss.

Conversely, the Life Saving Service report for 1879 stated that on February 27, 1879 the three-masted schooner *David H. Tolck* was stranded on the bar off Long Beach, New Jersey with eleven aboard of whom five were lost. Subsequent investigations revealed that Keeper Martin of Station 19 failed to act aggressively at the outset of the wreck resulting in the loss of five seamen. Keeper Martin was removed from the service.

Above: The British barque *Minmaneuth* aground on the south shore of Nantucket on July 30, 1873. The ship was carrying 4,000 bags of coffee from Rio de Janeiro to Boston. She was floated three days later after they unloaded 1,000 bags of coffee onto the beach. *Photo courtesy of Charles F. Sayle, Sr.* **Below:** The *City of Hartford* destroyed the railroad bridge across the Connecticut River at Middletown, about 15 miles below Hartford on the night of March 29, 1876. The ship struck the drawbridge on the port bow before carrying away the span. This accident resulted in new regulations to the effect that closed draws and fixed spans must show red lights. *Photo courtesy of the Steamship Historical Society of America.*

One of the strangest stories is the mystery of the Norwegian bark *Columbia*. From time to time, tales of dangerous sea monsters inhabiting the ocean depths are related in the news reports. Usually they are associated with an over indulgence of grog and are passed over. The *Columbia*, a wooden ship, was struck on the port bow early in the morning of September 4, 1879 at latitude 47°-32'N and longitude 43°-54'W. Quick investigation by Captain L.C.Larsen showed a huge hole in the bow and the ship was taking on water. The Captain and crew looked over the side of the ship and saw the water discolored with blood while the tail and fins of a huge monster were seen splashing about in the sea. The men on deck became frightened and the Captain, after seeing the water rising in the hold ordered his men to abandon ship. The bark sank about two hours after being struck and the monster was not seen again. The crewmen in the ship's boat were picked up later the same day by the steamship *P. Caland* and taken to Rotterdam, where the story was told. The monster, thought to be a whale, was described as an "array of tail and fin" reaching from the fore rigging to the main rigging of the vessel which was of 462 tons register or about 135' long. What little was seen of its back was much too round for that of a whale as was attested to by the crew. The story ends with the statement: "Captain Larsen is a very respectable looking mariner, with white hair and whiskers, and the honest smile which illuminates his face while he tells his unprecedented fish story would be to many sufficient proof of his veracity."

Business in the early part of the decade was booming. This was followed by a depression in 1874 caused by overexpansion and overspeculation by industry, and it lasted until 1879. There was widespread hunger and suffering. Wages were reduced, crime went up and the New York stock exchange closed for ten days because of the price collapse. In 1875 there were a half million unemployed in the country. Shipping suffered along with the rest of the country and Congress set up a subsidy for ships carrying the mail.

On May 10, 1876, President Ulysses S. Grant opened a Centenial Exposition in Philadelphia, and over 100,000 people attended. At the exposition the United States Life Saving Service set up a Life Saving Station which was later to be located at Cape May, New Jersey. The station was completely equipped with all of the apparatus, furniture and appliances for display purposes. The station, as described in the annual report, was visited by a multitude of people, including foreign visitors interested in nautical affairs. Among the foreigners were several officers of Life Saving Institutions in other countries. Also in evidence at the exposition was a display by the United States Lighthouse Board of models and drawings of lighthouses, buoys, fog horns, models of lightships and the superstructure of an actual lighthouse to be set up in Delaware Bay after the exposition. The Lighthouse service was one of the oldest agencies in the country and would in later years become part of the United States Coast Guard.

The Lighthouse service was similar in type of service to that of the Life Savers. Long days and nights with hours of boredom interrupted by hours of rescue efforts that ended in success or failure. Lighthouse Keepers, sometimes called "Wickies," because by day they spent long hours cleaning the oil burning lamps, were themselves sometimes called on to save men from ships wrecked nearby. Many were decorated with gold medals for their services. The annual report of the United States Lighthouse Board addressed to the Secretary of the Treasury was usually read by the lower echelons of the service in order to help justify their tedious existence. The months at a lonely outpost, keeping the lights burning at night and the fog horns blaring during thick weather was more than enough to wear out the most stout-hearted individual. Whenever a lighthouse Keeper might tire from his monotonous duties, a quick perusal of the annual report might lift his spirits. An example of this, in excerpts from the annual report of 1873 states: "Every shipwreck which occurs enhances the cost of transportation, and, therefore affects the interests of the producer. But it is not alone in view of its economical effects that the lighthouse system is to be regarded. It is a life preserving establishment, founded on the principles of Christian benevolence. None can appreciate so well the value of a proper system of this kind as he who has been exposed for weeks and perhaps months to the perils of the ocean, and is approaching in the darkness of night perhaps a lee shore. He looks then, with anxious gaze, for the friendly light which is to point the way amid treacherous rocks and sunken shoals to a haven of safety. Or it may be in mid-day, when observations cannot be had, the sun and coast being hid by

The *Atlantic* disaster on Mars Head which occurred on April 1, 1873, near Halifax, Nova Scotia. The vessel ran up on the rocks near Cape Prospect, turned over, and sank by the stern. There were 562 persons lost, mostly women and children. *Photo courtesy of the Public Archives of Nova Scotia.*

dense fogs, such as imperil navigation on our northern and western coasts. He then listens with breathless silence for the sound of the fog-trumpet which shall insure his position and give him the desired direction of his course.

"A light, for example, which has been regularly visible from a tower from night to night and from year to year cannot be suffered to fail for a single night, or even for a single hour, without danger of casualties of the most serious character. A failure of such a light to send forth its expected ray, is, as it were, a breach of a solemn promise, which may allure the confiding mariner to an untimely death or a disastrous shipwreck."

In those days, this stimulating prose usually had the desired effect in restoring the "esprit de corps" to the lighthouse Keeper. The message was not only meant to insure the enthusiasm of the men of the service, it had a "to whom it may concern" perspective for any of those who might become interested and especially those in the Government Service who might be connected with the appropriation of funds to underwrite expenditures of this type. Or, as we say in the 20th century, a better job of the "hard sell."

The worst single shipwreck around the New England area in the 1870's was the White Star liner *Atlantic* which went ashore on April 1, 1873, on Mars Head at Cape Prospect, Nova Scotia, during a heavy gale. There were 952 persons aboard the steamer. 562 of these were drowned, mostly women and children. The ship from Liverpool to New York was reported to be short of coal and was attempting to make Halifax harbor to replenish her bunkers. The vessel missed Sambro lighthouse and went ashore on the rocks at Mars Head. The heavy seas smashed the ship on the ledges and the hull turned over and sank by the stern after her boilers exploded, leaving only part of the bow and the masts out of water. Survivors clung to the rigging and clustered in the bow until help came from shore. Most of the passengers and crewmen that were saved were helped by the men from shore in small boats, without whom probably all hands would have been lost.

In other news of the decade, Alexander Graham Bell perfected the telephone in 1877, and in 1879 Thomas Alva Edison invented the electric light. Progress and the industrial revolution moved along rapidly in the United States. Woolworth opened the first five cent store in June of 1879. News from the western sections of the country was grim. In July of 1877, the latest word from the Idaho battle fields reported that Indians were still on the warpath as Federal troops were trying to herd them on to reservations.

CHAPTER TWO

In the decade of the 1880's American shipping was on the decline. Foreign competition had a weakening effect on the merchant marine. American exporters sent their freight abroad in the most economical hulls available. Capital formerly invested in shipping was being diverted into other industries on land which would employ more people and bring higher profits. Industrialist John D. Rockefeller formed the Standard Oil Company trust in 1882. In 1882 a French company began digging the Panama canal, and at the same time a fight was building in the United States Congress to lower tariffs. Most of the Congressmen were opposed, as the large sums being collected provided a huge surplus for Congress to spend.

In a review of marine folklore, one of the notable oddities was the sailor's superstitions. These beliefs were born in the age of sail and have been carried on through the years establishing customs that exist today. . . Never sail on Friday . . . Red sky at night, sailor's delight - Red sky in the morning, sailors take warning . . . Mermaids, Davy Jones' locker, the Flying Dutchman and blue paint are a few of the good or bad luck theories. A later entry in the mysteries is the highly imaginative "Bermuda Triangle." In the early 1880's the ship *St. Lawrence* was believed to be haunted. The Captain thought his ship unlucky and possessed of the devil because suicide, attempted murder and typhoons beset his vessel on a passage across the ocean. Modern mariners sail with scientific exactness and rely less and less on old sailors' tales but the magic is still there, and it is a part of sea lore to this day.

One of the old legends is about mermaids. A creature with the tail of a fish and the body of a woman. These girls must have lured the ship onto the rocks and wrecked her to get the beauty aids for their hair. *Reproduction from an old advertisement.*

Above: The steamer *Rhode Island,* built in 1873 was wrecked at Bonnet Point, at the west entrance to Narragansett Bay in 1880. The engine and parts of the superstructure were removed and used in the construction of the new (below) *Rhode Island* in 1882. The steamer hull was abandoned in later years and the hull was rebuilt as a six-masted schooner called the *Dovreffeld.* **Opposite:** The *Dovreffeld* is shown sunk at Stapleton, Staten Island, New York in 1917. She was raised and later was lost off Cape Hatteras, North Carolina in 1919.

← *The Dovrefjeld*   *Photo from the collection of Paul C. Morris, Nantucket, Massachusetts.*

There was an appalling disaster on March 4, 1881 when the Italian bark *Ajace* of Genoa, 566 tons with a crew of 14 men was wrecked on Rockaway Shoals, Long Island, N.Y., near Coney Island. During a severe gale the ship struck the shoal, and her crew gathered around the after cabin and began to pray to the Madonna. The storm grew worse and some of the men started to commit suicide by slashing their throats with knives. A huge wave broke the ship into pieces. Pietro Sala, an Austrian, clung to the cabin roof which had been torn from the hull and was floating. Other members of the crew were in the water swimming and trying to attain the roof but they were so debilitated by loss of blood that Sala was the only survivor. When he was spotted by the Life Savers of the Coney Island station, they launched their surfboat and rowed out in towering waves and rescued him from his precarious perch and brought him ashore. He was treated for exposure, and then he related the story of the 13 Italian crewmen killing themselves and the bloody mess that occurred during the wreck of the ship.

An example of outstanding work by a Life Saving crew took place on January 10, 1883, on the beach at Orleans on Cape Cod, Massachusetts. A heavy northeast gale was blowing during a blinding snowstorm, and a tremendous sea was breaking on the beach and crashing against the bank. The German bark *Friedricke,* 434 tons, out of Pillau, Prussia, for Portland, Maine, struck the outer bar on Nauset Beach, 500 yards south of the Life Saving Station. The stranding was witnessed by a member of the Life Saving crew who immediately alerted the station.

The Life Savers quickly went into action and dragged their beach cart through deep snow drifts on the sand swales behind the dunes to the edge of the bank at the scene of the wreck and fired a shot line across the fore yard and jibboom. In thirty minutes the entire crew of eleven men were saved, one by one across the tumbling field of breakers by the breeches buoy and taken to the station for dry clothes and hot food. The ship was a total wreck, but the cargo of rags was salvaged. The details in the annual report of the Life Saving Service included "good service" at the wreck of the *Friedricke.*

Above: This disaster scene depicts the collision between the steamboats *Narraganset* and *Stonington,* both of the Stonington line. The Currier and Ives prints were very popular in the 1880's. The *Narraganset* caught fire and burned. Fog was the cause of the accident that took about fifty lives in Long Island Sound on June 11, 1880. *Photo reproduction courtesy of the Peabody Museum of Salem.* **Below:** On March 27, 1882, the *Thomas Cornell* was wrecked on Danskammer Point just north of Marlborough, New York, on the Hudson River. The steamer was picking her way up river in dense fog patches when the accident occurred at about 8:30 p.m. The bow plowed up on the rocks, knocking down trees and tearing out bottom planking. The vessel was later hauled off the point, but the damage was so heavy that it was decided not to rebuild her, and she was abandoned. The hull was later made into two barges. *Photo courtesy of Donald C. Ringwald collection, Albany, New York.*

Early in the morning of January 18, 1884, the Boston-Savanah steamer *City of Columbus,* hit the rocks at Devil's Bridge on the western tip of Martha's Vineyard Island. Out of the 87 passengers and 45 crewmen, 103 people died, many from exposure while in the rigging waiting for rescue. *Photo courtesy of the Vineyard Gazette, Edgartown, Massachusetts.*

The most notable shipwreck in the 1880's in New England was the loss of the *City of Columbus,* 1,991 tons. The steamer left Boston on January 17, 1884, bound for Savanah, Georgia, with 45 crewmen and 87 passengers headed for the winter in Florida. Early the next morning the captain made an error in dead reckoning and came to grief on Devil's Bridge off Gay Head on Martha's Vineyard island. The ship ran up on submerged rocks and stove a hole in her bottom. The ship did not hit very hard and her captain believed that the damage was minimal; so, he decided to back her off. The vessel had suffered a fatal blow when she fetched up on the ledges. When she backed off, water poured into the hold and she settled quickly carrying many people to their deaths.

Many people drowned in their cabins still in their night clothes. Some climbed into the rigging and died from exposure in the icy January night air. There were only 29 survivors out of the 132 persons on board. Many of those saved were brought ashore by volunteers of the Massachusetts Humane Society. Gay Head Indians manned the society boats and ventured out in rough waters to save those they could. Among the survivors was Captain S. E. Wright. A court of inquiry found him negligent and revoked his license.

Immigration reached a high point during this period. More people came to the United States than had ever come before or since. In the years 1880 to 1889 over five million foreign born arrived in the United States to begin a new life. An ever present danger was a heavily laden ship getting into trouble. The French steamship *Scotia,* 2496 tons, out of Naples, Italy for New York City with 872 persons aboard stranded on the outer bar opposite the Blue Point, Long Island station on March 25, 1887. With the aid of the adjacent stations, Lone Hill and Bellport, all 830 passengers were landed in two days with the breeches buoy and lifeboats. This was a formidable task to perform without any injuries or loss of life.

The stranding brought illegal overloading charges against the *Scotia.* The vessel was only licensed to carry 486 passengers. There were charges by the immigrants of poor food, while some of the male passengers complained of being made to work shoveling coal in the boiler rooms. A passenger later died in the hospital from exposure and weakness. The ship was pulled off the bar a month later, but part of the cargo was lost.

Above: Late in the evening of August 22, 1884, the *U.S.S. Tallapoosa*, a sidewheel Navy steamer, was rammed and sunk in Vineyard Sound by the coal laden schooner *James S. Lowell* of Bath, Maine. The accident occurred on a clear night, and witnesses claimed that both vessels saw the lights of the other. The *Lowell* and other vessels picked up the crew of the steamer, which went down in ten minutes. Three of the crew of the Naval vessel were lost. The ship was raised and repaired in the New York Naval Shipyard. *Photo by Baldwin Coolidge, courtesy of the Society for the Preservation of New England Antiquities, Boston, Mass.* **Below:** On July 18, 1886, the Steamer *Gate City* ran aground on Naushon Island, southwest of Cape Cod, Massachusetts, in dense fog. The Boston-Savanah vessel was loaded with watermelons. The unfortunate vessel with a history of many mishaps ran aground just a few miles from Devil's Bridge where her sister ship the *City of Columbus* was wrecked on January 17, 1884. Her bow, with a rock piercing the hull, rested 150 feet off shore with her stern in 25 feet of water. Thousands of watermelons were dumped overboard to lighten the vessel. She was refloated a week later. *Photo courtesy of the Mariners Museum, Newport News, Virginia.*

A derelict schooner being towed by a Revenue Cutter. *Drawing by Paul C. Morris, Nantucket, Mass.*

Because of the perils of ship travel, numerous safety proposals were offered, and some were accepted while others were rejected. There was a proposal in 1888 for a Government vessel to dispose of wrecks (derelicts) at sea in the shipping lanes of the United States. It was proposed that Atlantic steamers should not be obliged to stop and destroy floating wrecks in the sea lane approaches to U.S. ports. Wrecked and abandoned vessels were usually blown up by the United States Navy or Revenue Cutters. Also, the hulks should be habitually removed so as not to be a peril to ocean navigation such as found in the most traveled steamer routes on our side of the Atlantic.

A peculiar idea was offered to station lightships every 200 miles all the way across the Atlantic Ocean. The plan called for sea lanes to be set up on either side of the string of ships and that westbound traffic would use the northern lanes and that eastbound traffic to follow the southern lanes. This was to insure that there would be no collisions at sea and that ship travel would be made safer. There were no answers to questions about fog banks, when traffic would become lost out of the sea lanes in a 3,000 mile wide ocean. There is an old story down Maine about an old Indian who, upon seeing the Federal Government spending large sums of money on lighthouses and fog horns, said: "UGH! white man waste much wampum on lights, horns, and bells and fog still rolls in."

A unique phenomenon was described in the 1884 annual report of the United States Life Saving Service: "At many points on our sea coast and on the shores of the Great Lakes, the beach sand has, in small tracts, very curious properties. In certain places the dry sand between the water line and extreme high tide yields a peculiar sound when struck obliquely by the foot, or even when stroked by the hand; at the same time a tingling sensation can sometimes be felt in the toes or in the fingers. The sounds produced by friction, as described, resemble somewhat the distant barking of a dog, and may be represented by the syllable *groosh*. They are unlike and louder than the ordinary grating noise caused by wagon wheels in deep sand, and when once heard are easily recognized. Under favorable circumstances they may be heard one hundred feet. Only dry sand has this property, and hence damp weather obscures the sounds. Sands having this peculiarity are sometimes called singing sands."

Above: The Boston-Bangor steamer *Katahdin* had a close call on the night of January 9, 1886, when she ran into a gale off Cape Porpoise and battled high seas for ten hours. The gale did damage to the sides of the vessel and her crew had to take her freight, furniture, and anything else that would burn and feed the fires to keep the ship afloat and underway. She limped into Portsmouth, New Hampshire, the morning after. **Below:** The St. John, New Brunswick bark *Annie C. Maguire* was driven up on the ledges, 100 yards from the Portland Head Lighthouse. The vessel was wrecked during gale winds and driving snow on Christmas Eve, December 24, 1886. The crew was saved, but the ship was lost. *Photos from the marine collection of Frank E. Claes, Orland, Maine.*

Above: The Steamer *Empire State* was lying in state in winter storage at the railroad pier at Bristol, Rhode Island, when she caught fire late on the evening of May 13, 1887. Two men, shipkeepers on board, barely escaped the flames. The fire completely gutted the ship, and the remains sank beside the pier. *Photo courtesy of the Society for the Preservation of New England Antiquities, Boston, Massachusetts.* **Below:** A collision at sea in thick fog. On May 21, 1887, the schooner *Messenger* from Salem, Massachusetts collided with the ship *Sooloo,* seventy miles east-southeast of the South Shoals lightship. The *Sooloo* lost her topmasts and spars and suffered other damage and had to be towed into Boston. After this incident she was converted to a coal barge. *Photo courtesy of the Peabody Museum of Salem.*

Above: The palatial steamer *Bristol,* 2,960 tons, 240 state rooms, built in 1886, one of the grand steamers of the Fall River line, burned at the pier at Newport, Rhode Island, on the night of December 30, 1888. She caught fire from fat boiling over in the galley. Her sister ship, the *Providence,* is shown behind her on the morning after the fire. *Photo courtesy of the Peabody Museum of Salem* **Below:** The three-masted schooner *H.C. Higginson* stranded near Nantasket Beach, Massachusetts at 8 p.m. on November 25, 1888 during a northeast gale. Life Savers from the North Situate station could not reach the wreck in the storm. However, the Massachusetts Humane Society crew in the lifeboat *Nantasket* under the command of Captain Joshua James of Hull, reached the schooner and saved five of the crew. Two men had been washed overboard earlier, and one man froze to death in the rigging. Captain James and his crew were decorated for their rescue of the five men. The vessel was later towed to port in a damaged condition. *Photo from the collection of Richard M. Boonisar.*

The famous surfboat *Nantasket* and her equally famous crew of Hull, volunteers for the Massachusetts Humane Society led by Captain Joshua James. Captain James is standing in the after part of the boat behind the man with his hands on the steering oar. Their boat which weathered many storms and rescued countless men is now housed at the Hull Life Saving Museum in Hull, Massachusetts. *Photo from the collection of Richard M. Boonisar.*

One of the most famous New England Life Savers was Captain Joshua James of Hull, Massachusetts. Capt. James was a volunteer member of the Massachusetts Humane Society for forty years and on November 25-26, 1888, he and his men saved the lives of twenty-nine persons from four vessels wrecked on the Hull shores. The first was the schooner *Cox and Green* where nine men were removed by the breeches buoy. Then the schooner *Gertrude Abbot* became stranded off shore. Eight men were saved by the lifeboat. Then came the schooner *Bertha F. Walker.* Again by lifeboat, seven men were rescued. The last of the group was the schooner *H. C. Higginson,* bound from Hillsboro, New Brunswick, to Newburgh, New York, with a cargo of rock plaster, when she lost some of her sails in a storm. She anchored off Scituate but her chains parted, driving her ashore at Nantasket Beach. The heavy seas inundated her hull and when the Life Savers arrived on the scene she was sunk with her decks awash 150 yards from shore with her crew clinging to life in the rigging.

Efforts by both the Life Saving Service crew and the Massachusetts Humane Society volunteers to establish a life line between the wrecked schooner and shore by use of the breeches buoy failed, and at that time the Humane Society boat crew under Captain James arrived on the scene with a twelve-oared surfboat, and they launched in the stormy seas. The boat reached the schooner and removed the five remaining crewmen from the rigging. Two men had been washed overboard and another had died from exposure. For their gallant efforts, Captain James and his crew were awarded gold and silver life saving medals. The schooner was salvaged and refloated later, but the cargo was lost. In 1889 the Life Saving Service built a station at Stony Beach and selected Joshua James as the Keeper. Capt. James continued in his illustrious career of Life Saving until he was 75 years of age. He died on the beach while drilling his men in 1902.

Sandy Hook in a fog.
N.J.   May 7. 1887.
No. 2. U.S.L.S.S.
Dear Col Shaw.
We have had a thick fog and East wind for 3 days.

Artist and writer Peter Cameron spent a few days at Sandy Hook Life Saving Station in New Jersey in May of 1887. He wrote a letter to his friend Col. Shaw relating his experiences while at the station and headed up his letter with this unique illustration. The letter described conditions at the station and his association with Keeper Patterson and his 10-year old son, watching for shipwrecks, patrolling the beach in dense fog for a distance of five miles, and his plans for a future illustrated magazine article on the Life Saving Service. *Letter loaned by Richard M. Boonisar, Norwell, Massachusetts.*

One of the more unusual stories occurred on the Maine coast on June 27, 1889 when at about midnight the three-masted schooner *William C. French* went aground in dense fog on Glover's Rock, six miles west south west of the Hunniwell's Beach Life Saving Station at the mouth of the Kennebec River. At the time of the grounding it was high water of a moon tide and therefore efforts to refloat her later met with no success. The *French* was of 408 tons, built at Newburyport, Massachusetts in 1883 and because of her position, was declared a total loss. The ship was auctioned off to the highest bidder. The A. Sewall & Co. of Bath, Maine, bought her as she was, jacked her up and built a new ways under her and launched the schooner as they would a new vessel. After they refitted her for sea, they renamed her the *Dicky Bird* because she had perched on land.

The decade was an eventful one. Following the depression of the 1870's, money was again abundant and employment was on the upswing. In 1881 the American Red Cross was formed in Washington, D.C., to help persons in need during natural disasters. In 1883, the longest suspension bridge in the world opened over the East River in New York City. The Brooklyn Bridge cost fifteen million dollars to build and was 5,989 feet long. In October of 1886 the Statue of Liberty was dedicated on Bedloe's Island in New York harbor.

CHAPTER THREE

America's growth into an industrial giant went forward in the 1890's. The vast expansionism was caused by dramatic increases in her wealth, population and commerce. United States manufacturers had caught up with domestic demands and were seeking foreign markets for their products, accumulating in bulging warehouses. In the years 1889 through 1890 six more western states had been admitted, bringing the total now to forty-four. The merchant marine continued its decline. American ships were laid up because British vessels were carrying the freight at lower rates. Mr. William M. Ivins spoke to the United States Senate Commerce Committee on April 28, 1892 and outlined the reasons for deterioration. British labor costs in building and manning their ships were cheaper. American wages were about 25% higher than their British counterparts for the same labor. Later a bill was introduced in the United States Congress calling for rehabilitation of the merchant marine by subsidizing the industry. The legislation was camouflaged by adding pennies to various costs in shipping but when multiplied out the costs ballooned into millions. John Codman of New York called the American shipping industry "Bounty Beggars" in their support for subsidies, bountys and subventions for United States ships, and he recommended defeat of the bill.

Coastal shipping enjoyed the protection of a law prohibiting foreign ships from engaging in commerce along the United States coasts. All domestic cargoes had to be carried in our own bottoms. One popular type of vessel for this trade was the four-masted schooner. Under ideal conditions, they were good money makers with the carrying capacity of a ship without the expense of a large crew and the maintenance of a square rigger. An important feature of the large schooner was the donkey engine. This engine was used to raise the sails, heave in the anchor, help handle cargo, run the bilge pumps, and save many hours of hard work usually done by the crew. This extra help on board enabled the vessel to sail with small crews; therefore, economic operation.

There were a few flaws in the four-masters. Taller masts tended to carry greater strains, and the hulls suffered considerable stresses when empty causing hogging. The average life span of one of the large coal carriers was about fifteen years. In the early 1890's the large sailing schooners were being lost at an alarming rate causing the underwriters to become skeptical about issuing policies on these ships. In 1890 some insurance companies declined to write policies on four-masters with centerboards. Their flat bottoms tended to pound in a seaway and suffer dangerous hull twists while rolling in heavy swells. They continued to sail however into the 1902's.

On November 29, 1893, a four-masted schooner, the *Louise H. Randall,* was wrecked in a storm off Smiths Point on Long Island, New York. Those on board, including the captain's wife, for whom the vessel was named, had to climb into the rigging and remain there for almost two days before rescue could be effected. The vessel lay six-hundred yards off shore with heavy seas running. Life Savers on shore were unable to reach the eleven battered survivors hanging onto life in those terrible conditions.

Above: The two-masted schooner *Mexican* bound from New York City to Bucksport, Maine, with a cargo of coal and was wrecked during a northwest gale on October 17, 1890, at Ipswich Bay, Mass., near the Davis Neck Life Saving station. Life Savers rescued the crew of four. *Photo courtesy of Library of Congress, Washington, D.C.* **Below:** The Iron Steamboat Company's steamer *Cepheus* struck a hidden obstruction on August 12, 1892 near Coney Island, New York City. She suffered a large hole in her hull. The Captain ran her into shoal water at Norton Point to prevent her from sinking in deep water. The ship was 578 tons, 213.5' long and was raised six days later by salvagers from the Chapman Derrick & Wrecking Company and towed to a Brooklyn dock. *Photo courtesy of Paul C. Morris, Nantucket, Massachusetts.*

The steam salvage vessel *I. J. Merritt* arrived the next day and saved all eleven persons and took them back to New York where they were hospitalized, and all survived. A New York paper ran an editorial the next day criticizing the Life Saving Service for not having proper equipment and apparatus to effect an immediate rescue for persons aboard vessels caught off shore beyond present limits. They lauded the discipline and bravery of the Life Saving men but warned the authorities that a lesson had been learned in the loss of the schooner and improved apparatus should be obtained to serve this type of accident better. The writer proposed stronger rockets, both aboard ship and on land but unfortunately fifty years would pass before Igor Sikorsky perfected the modern helicopter which was to be the improved apparatus called for in the news story.

It was common practice in those days, when a ship was wrecked on shore, for the local citizens to offer their hospitality to the survivors but there were exceptions. In late May of 1894, the British cargo steamer *Calitro,* Sunderland to Baltimore, with a cargo of cement, steaming in dense fog ran on the rocks at Horse Cove, about fifty miles north of St. Johns, Newfoundland. The ship was badly damaged and her crew left in their lifeboats to seek aid. They rowed to Grates Cove and told the townspeople of the disaster. About one hundred of the local men returned to the scene of the wreck and looted the ship of everything that could be stolen and would not even allow the crew to come back aboard to claim their personal belongings. The wreckers removed the cabin fittings, saloon furniture, ships gear, ropes and chains, and took hatchets to wood panels and stole all of the ships stores. Captain J.M. Storm, his wife and the crew, 29 in all, were returned to St. Johns by the steamer *Ingraham* where the captain brought charges against the wreckers. The steamer and her cargo were valued at $300,000.

The remote residents of Newfoundland had a reputation for being pirates when ships came ashore and Canadian officials were indifferent to complaints by ship owners of the outrageous state of affairs on the Newfoundland coastline. At this point in history the only industry practiced in the province was fishing; so that a vessel tossed ashore was a bonus for the natives.

The New York Times later editorialized against this behavior and proposed some harsh action. "The only course that can be suggested is for a United States or an English gunboat to go up into that region and argue with the resident savages in exactly the manner that reformed the habits, if not the morals, of the piratical Moroccans. If only shelling a village or two can convince those so-called fishermen that to intimidate captains and rob ships is no longer stylish, then the village or two ought to be shelled just as soon as a few naval men can be spared from Halifax or Bar Harbor."

Vessels coming into New York harbor were obliged to hire a pilot to con the ship safely into port. It was usual for a pilot to board a vessel out at sea but most captains stipulated that there be no charges for off shore pilotage. A few dollars saved would endear the captain to his owners but the pilot was not responsible for the ship until it entered pilot waters. False economy was shown in the case of the British steamer *Persian Monarch* which ran aground off Eastport, Long Island, on May 2, 1894. Pilot Thomas Jackson was aboard but he had not taken the con. He did however, notice that the ship was in danger of going aground and advised the quartermaster at the wheel to sheer off a couple of points. Without orders from the captain the man could not change course so the pilot went below and reported to Captain Bristow: "You had better keep off shore a little more captain," he said. "I know this coast pretty well," was the response. "Well you'll know it better directly," replied Pilot Jackson, and he was right. Later the British Consul charged responsibility to the pilot, but it was declined and Captain Bristow had his certificate suspended. The ship was aground for two days.

Another depression and stock market crash hit the country in 1893-94. Employment went down and prices went up and many businessmen failed as they were unable to get bank loans to pay their bills. In 1897, automobiles were the talk of the nation. Detroit began building the horseless carriages which ultimately would become the most important factor in the United States economy. Detroit was a natural locus for automobile manufacturing as it had been a carriage building center with all of the skilled tradesmen, and was close to iron ore for steel for engine building which would usher in the machine age for most Americans. Henry Ford and Ransom Olds began to build production lines, and the automobile was on its way.

On the evening of September 28, 1892, the Metropolitan liner *H.M. Whitney* was headed out of Boston Harbor for New York City when she was struck on the starboard bow by the *S.S. Ottoman* which was entering the harbor at the time. A mix-up in whistle signals was blamed for the accident. The *Whitney* was salvaged later and went back into service. *Photo by M.L. Stebbins, courtesy of the Society for the Preservation of New England Antiquities, Boston, Massachusetts.*

Above: On the night of November 30, 1892, the Quebec bark *Kate Harding* was battling a gale off Cape Cod, Massachusetts when she stranded on the outer bar off Truro. The Lifesavers from the Highland and High Head stations removed her crew of ten by the breeches buoy. The vessel was a total loss. *Photo by Henry K. Cummings, Orleans, Mass.* **Below:** An early schooner wreck on Nantucket. Three girls, a dog, and an elder friend find the scene idyllic for a summer photograph. *Photo from the collection of Paul C. Morris, Nantucket, Massachusetts.*

Above: On March 25, 1893, the German Oil tanker *Gluckauf* was lost in the fog and went ashore on Fire Island Beach opposite Sayville, Long Island, New York. The vessel could not be pulled off the beach, and wreckers boarded her. After a month the ship was abandoned and her loss was set at $125,000. The *Gluckauf* was the prototype of today's giant oil tankers, the first of her kind. The engines aft and tanks forward, the general layout was similar to the modern-day tanker. She had square sails on her foremast and fore and aft sails on her two other masts. This photograph was taken about two years after her wreck and the hull had become a tourist attraction. Her name on her bows, *Gluckauf* in big brass letters a foot long meant "good luck," or "lucky one" - the irony of fate. *Photo courtesy of the Suffolk Marine Museum, West Sayville, New York.* **Below:** The *Jason,* a full-rigged English ship, passed Cape Cod on December 5, 1893. She nearly made it around the end of the Cape, but a fierce northeast storm wrecked her on Pamet bar in Truro. Twenty-four men lost their lives. One man made it ashore through the wind-lashed surf. The ship with a cargo of jute was a total loss. *Photo by Henry K. Cummings, Orleans, Massachusetts.*

Above: Sometimes old age was a deciding factor for the demise of a ship. The steamer *City of Boston,* built in 1861, awaits the ship breakers on Nut Island in Boston Harbor. She steamed for over 30 years in the sheltered waters of Long Island Sound between New York City and New London and Norwich, Connecticut. *Photo from the marine collection of Frank E. Claes.* **Below:** On April 13, 1894, the schooner *Jennie M. Carter* stranded on Salisbury Beach, Massachusetts, during stormy weather. Life savers boarded the wreck and saved a few articles - sextant, compass and an aneroid barometer for the owners. All hands were lost and the bodies of three sailors washed ashore on the north shore. *Photo courtesy of the Peabody Museum of Salem.*

Above: A fire of unknown origin gutted the full-rigged ship *Gen. Knox* at pier 19 on the East River in New York City on August 18, 1894. Half of the cargo of kerosene, resin, creosote, and turpentine had been loaded aboard the ship when she caught fire. New York City firemen poured water on the blazing vessel, flooding the ship, and she sank at the dock. The fire was extinguished but the ship was a loss. She was raised later only to become a schooner barge. *Photo from the collection of Paul C. Morris, Nantucket, Massachusetts.* **Below:** On January 5, 1895, the schooner *Job H. Jackson, Jr.* was wrecked near Peaked Hills Bars, Cape Cod, Massachusetts during a gale. The vessel had lost her sails and had become unmanageable. Life Saving crews from the Peaked Hills Bars and High Head stations launched a boat in high seas and effected the rescue of the crew of nine. Some of the crew were badly frostbitten. The schooner was a total loss. *Photo by Henry K. Cummings, Orleans, Massachusetts.*

Above: On February 8, 1895, the schooner *Louis V. Place* stranded one half mile east of the Moriches Life Saving Station on Long Island, New York, during heavy seas and gale winds. The vessel was described as a floating iceberg. The crew climbed into the rigging to await rescue. On the second day, six men succumbed to exposure before the Life Savers could get a boat out through mountainous surf to rescue the two survivors left. The two men saved were carried to the station for treatment. One survivor, William Stevens said: "Well, it was a rough experience. The masts of the vessel swayed back and forth all day, and every moment I expected would be our last. But I don't seem to feel it much. With a pan of baked beans and a good smoke I could have held out for a number of hours longer." The schooner was 735 tons, bound from Baltimore to New York City with a cargo of coal. S.J. Nelson, the other survivor, later died from the ordeal. **Below:** A close up look at the ice-covered rigging. *Photos by Anderson, courtesy of the Suffolk Marine Museum, West Sayville, New York.*

Above: The Steamer *Venetian* lying atop a ledge in Boston Harbor, split in the middle. The ship, with a full cargo, went aground on March 2, 1895. The cargo was lightered off, but the hull became a total loss. *Photo courtesy of Mariners Museum, Newport News, Virginia.* **Below:** The tidal flow and passage of time reduced the *Venetian* to a marine billboard advertising boots. *Photo courtesy of Peabody Museum of Salem.*

Above: The Sound steamer *Continental* ran up on Hog's Back Reef on Ward's Island near Hell Gate, New York, in dense fog just after midnight on March 31, 1895. Her 80 passengers were retired when the accident occurred. The passengers were removed the next morning. The ship was ultimately pulled off the reef and went back into service between New York City and New Haven, Connecticut. **Below:** The *S.S. Olinda* went on the rocks off Goose Hummock on the south side of Fishers Island, New York, on June 11, 1895, in thick fog. She had on board a Fall River pilot, and he ran the vessel too close to shore. Her cargo of cork and empty barrels was saved. A storm broke the vessel in two, and she stayed there. *Photos from the collection of Paul C. Morris, Nantucket, Massachusetts.*

Above: In 1895, accidents to summer boaters on Dorchester Bay in Boston prompted the United States Life Saving Service to establish a floating station in the bay. It was unique; since most of the Life Saving Stations were closed in the summer. The City Point station was manned from May to October and then laid up in winter. The above photo was made shortly after the station went into operation. *Photo courtesy of The Society for the Preservation of New England Antiquities, Boston, Massachusetts.* **Below:** On February 4, 1896, the British Steamer *Lamington* stranded on the Great South Beach of Eastern Long Island, 4½ miles south of Patchogue. The grounding occurred at seven o'clock in the evening during thick, stormy weather. Life Savers from three stations gathered at the scene but because of the weather they could not rescue the crew of 24 until the following day. Tugs, and wreckers spent almost three weeks trying to save the vessel and were finally successful on the 26th, pulling her off the bar. The cargo of fruit was lost. *Photo by Anderson, courtesy of Suffolk Marine Museum, West Sayville, New York.*

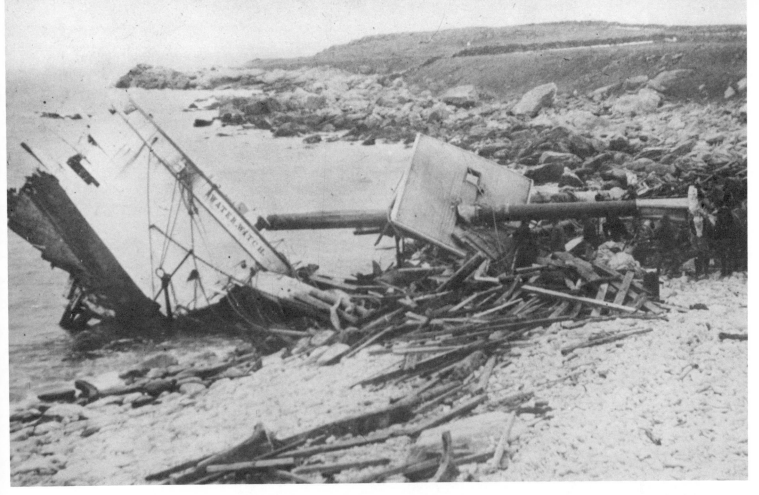

Above: The brig *Water Witch* was wrecked on the coast of Rhode Island on March 19, 1896, while battling high seas and heavy gale winds. The vessel broke up soon after coming aground. The crew managed to land in their boat but failed to save any personal property. The ship carried a cargo of logwood, most of which was lost. *Photo from the National Archives, Washington, D.C.* **Below:** On July 4, 1896, a tow consisting of the steamer *Nottingham* and three coal laden barges stranded late in the evening off Southhampton Beach near Shinnecock Inlet, Long Island, New York, in dense fog. The tug managed to free herself and another barge but one barge, the *Central Railroad of New Jersey No. 6,* was hard aground. The third barge broke in half and was abandoned. Wreckers from the Chapman Wrecking Company managed to free the *C.R.R. of N.J. No. 6* a week later and she was towed to Providence, Rhode Island. *Photo from the collection of Paul C. Morris, Nantucket, Massachusetts.*

Above: On July 30, 1896, about one year after the *Olinda* (page 29) was wrecked, the steamer *Tillie* ran aground at the same place - the rocks off Goose Hummock on the south side of Fishers Island, New York. The ship was under charter and was loaded with sardines. Tugs pulled her off two days later. The ship was sunk later while carrying munitions to the army at Cuba. *Photo from the collection of Paul C. Morris, Nantucket, Massachusetts.* **Below:** The British barque *Corryvrechan* had a close call with disaster during a storm off the Massachusetts coast on January 28, 1897. After a voyage from the tropics the abrupt change in climate had a chilling effect on the crew, and they were unable to handle their ship. The vessel was anchored off Nantasket. Tugs and crews from Boston went to her aid and brought the storm-tattered ship into port. *Photo courtesy of the Peabody Museum of Salem.*

Above: The United States Lighthouse supply steamer *Armeria* was cruising in fog in East Penobscot Bay, Maine, on August 15, 1897, when she ran up on a large ledge of rocks north of Bradbury Island. The tide was high at the time, and there were rocks amidship. At low tide her stern was out of water. Wreckers had to use pontoons to float her on the 23rd. The United States steamers *Lilac* and *Myrtle* and tugs *Ralph Ross, Kate Jones* and *William Sprague,* pulled the *Armeria* off the rocks and towed her into Northwest Harbor. *Photo from the marine collection of Frank E. Claes, Orland, Maine.* **Below:** The steamer *Ulster* of the Saugerties Evening Line hard up on the bank of the Hudson River on November 12, 1897. A strange accident where the pilot had stomach seizures and let go of the wheel. The vessel yawed around and ran on the bank at full speed! She later sank by the stern. The ship was ultimately raised and repaired and returned to service on the river. Going by in the background is the steamer *Emeline* which appears on page 42 in another accident on the river. *Photo from the collection of Paul C. Morris, Nantucket, Massachusetts.*

The great gale of November 1898 caused hundreds of casualties. Among them was the schooner *Henry R. Tilton* which was blown ashore at Toddy Rocks 1½ miles west of the Point Allerton Life Saving Station, whose crew hurried to the scene, set up the breeches buoy, and brought the crew of seven ashore during the worst of the gale. The *Henry R. Tilton* was later refloated and sailed until she was lost off Cape Cod in 1912. *Photo courtesy of The Society for the Preservation of New England Antiquities, Boston, Massachusetts.*

The great storm of November 1898 destroyed the steamer *Portland* with the crew and passengers - nearly 200 people. The ship went down, with all hands, off Cape Cod. *Photo courtesy of the Peabody Museum of Salem.*

The most dangerous storm of the decade occurred on November 26 and 27, 1898. The two day hurricane went into the history books as the Portland Gale. The blizzard raged at full intensity for thirty-six hours, gradually abating on the third day. Seventy mile per hour winds lashed the entire New England coastline. The seas became higher as the storm gained in intensity. The oceanic turbulence tossed ships on shore like driftwood. The most noted wreck during the gale was that of the steamer *Portland* lost with all her crew and passengers. It was estimated that between 150 and 200 people were aboard the vessel when she foundered somewhere north of Peaked Hill Bars off Cape Cod.

The storm wrecked more ships than any other in the history of New England. There were many vessels that did not report, indicating a loss at sea. Miles of the coastline from Cape Cod to Portland, Maine were piled high with wreckage or disabled vessels, and the physical appearance of the shore line was altered by the wind and waves. Snow was measured in feet and all communications were cut off. All telephone lines off Cape Cod were severed, and news of the *Portland* wreckage ashore on the back side of the Cape was wired to France over the transatlantic cable in Orleans, and from there sent to New York over another cable, and thence to Boston.

In Provincetown harbor there were thirty vessels wrecked and many lives lost. Vineyard Haven harbor was devastated. Numerous schooners were piled up on shore and most of those in the harbor were sunk or badly damaged. In all, over 140 ships were sunk or wrecked in the great gale of November 26-27, 1898.

Above: During the great gale of November 1898, the American schooner *Albert L. Butler* came ashore at Peaked Hill Bars in Provincetown on Cape Cod. Three men were lost but the Life Savers succeeded in saving five of her crew during the worst of the storm. *Photo by Rosenthal, courtesy of Cape Cod Photos, Orleans, Massachusetts.* **Below:** Another victim of the storm was the fishing vessel *Juanita*. The fishing schooner came ashore at Cohasset, Massachusetts. *Photo by Stebbins, courtesy of the Society for the Preservation of New England Antiquities, Boston, Massachusetts*

Above: One victim of the gale was the pilot boat *Columbia.* The vessel was smashed up against a house at Scituate, Massachusetts. The four year old schooner was a total wreck. Her crew of five were all lost in the storm. Their bodies were found later on the beach near the vicinity of the wreck. *Photo courtesy of the Smithsonian Institute, Washington, D.C.* **Below:** The *Mertis H. Perry* was wrecked two miles northwest of the Brant Rock Life Saving Station in Marshfield, Massachusetts, on the morning of November 27th during the height of the great gale. Five of the fourteen men aboard lost their lives. The mountainous surf cast the fishing vessel far up on the beach, and the crewmen were able to crawl ashore over the jibboom which extended over the bank. The crew made their way to a farmhouse and were given shelter. The *Mertis H. Perry* was not discovered by the Life Savers until mid-afternoon. The schooner was a total loss. *Photo from the collection of Richard M. Boonisar, Norwell, Massachusetts.*

Above: On March 23, 1899, the British bark *La Escocesa* alongside the tug *McCaldin Bros.* was flipped over by a strong gust of wind in upper New York bay. Both the bark and the tug sank. A week later, salvage crews raised the two vessels. *Photo courtesy of Paul C. Morris, Nantucket, Massachusetts.* **Below:** The British steamer *Norseman* went aground on Tom Moore rock off Marblehead, Massachusetts, on March 19, 1899, in dense fog and high seas. About one hundred persons on board were removed by the breeches buoy. The damaged vessel was refloated a few days later. *Photo by Stebbins, courtesy of the Society for the Preservation of New England Antiquities, Boston, Massachusetts.*

Above: Two New Haven Line steamers collide in fog. The *Richard Peck* rammed the *C.H. Northam* in Long Island Sound on June 8, 1899. The *Northam* was beached to prevent sinking. Later refloated and repaired the vessel was back on the run in three weeks. *Photo from the collection of Paul C. Morris, Nantucket, Massachusetts.* **Below:** In the Atlantic, south of Newport, Rhode Island on August 2, 1899, the *Columbia* was in a trial race with *Defender,* and the race was abruptly halted by a broken mast on the *Columbia.* Cause of the fallen steel mast was reputed to be the port spreader, broken upward by the strain of the topmast shroud which caused the topmast to break off, collapsing the main mast. The yacht was towed to Bristol, Rhode Island and repaired. The *Columbia* successfully defended the America's Cup in three races in September 1899, against Sir Thomas Lipton's *Shamrock. Photo courtesy of the Society for the Preservation of New England Antiquities, Boston, Massachusetts.*

In October of 1899 the steamer *Cimbria* of the Bangor & Bar Harbor Steamboat Company, ran up on the rocks in the fog at Bass Harbor, Maine, on the southeast point of Mount Desert Island. She was pulled off badly damaged and had to be rebuilt. In the spring of 1900 she was re-launched with a new superstructure but minus her two masts. *Photo from the collection of Frank E. Claes, Orland, Maine.*

A bizarre incident occurred outside New York harbor on December 8, 1899, when an eight inch dummy shell fired from the ordnance proving grounds at Sandy Hook struck the New Jersey pilot boat *James Gordon Bennett* about a mile south of the Scotland Lighship and over four miles off the shores of New Jersey.

The shell hit the water and ricocheted over the port side of the vessel and struck the inside of the hull and continued through and out the starboard side. All damage was above the water line so there was no danger of sinking but it left the *Bennett* badly damaged. Fortunately there were no personal injuries on board, but the pilots were furious at being used as targets. Officials at the proving grounds attributed the accident to a bad bounce. A study turned up other instances in the past where vessels had been struck by shells from Sandy Hook and most mariners felt that it was time to remove the proving grounds from the shoreline adjacent to a major maritime traffic artery.

In February, 1898, there was a mysterious explosion aboard the battleship *Maine* while she was anchored at Havana harbor in Cuba. The ship sank immediately, and over 250 officers and men died. Both sides blamed the other for the act and in April the United States declared war on Spain. The United States won the war which lasted only until August and finally ended with the treaty of Paris.

CHAPTER FOUR

The turn of the century ushered in a new era for the country. In 1900 the value of the dollar was backed up by gold as the United States went on the gold standard. The population had grown to seventy-five million people, and Mr. J.P. Morgan formed the United States Steel Corporation. Fewer American merchant ships were seen on the worlds' oceans and the British merchant marine continued to thrive. The radio, or wireless, was in its infant stage, but the inventor Guglielmo Marconi had improved his equipment so that he was sending messages across the Atlantic Ocean. In 1903, ocean lanes were proposed for the transatlantic steamers. This was precipitated by fatal collisions in the North Atlantic. Panama gave the United States the rights to build a canal and the Wright Brothers were the first men to lift off in a powered airplane flight at Kill Devil Hill in Kittyhawk, North Carolina.

The domestic shipping of the country continued its growth in varied ways. During the decade shipbuilding in Maine was brisk and profitable. Nine six-masted schooners and thirty-eight five-masted schooners for the coal and lumber trades came down the ways - all within a ten year period. The average life of these wooden vessels was about 14 years, but seven of the five-masted schooners were wrecked within two years of their launching. The most dangerous position for one of these vessels was being caught off a lee shore during a gale. Many of these picturesque ships broke up in the surf, but most of them continued to make money for their owners into the 1920's. In 1902, a seven-masted giant with a steel hull was built in Quincy, Massachusetts. The *Thomas W. Lawson* was one of a kind with a vast measurement of 5,218 gross tons and she could carry 11,000 tons of coal.

There were, at times, strange reasons given for shipwrecks. Sailors related tall tales which authorities could not believe. Further investigation brought to light some drunken crewmen. Sailors would drink almost anything they could lay a hand to. Not always pure and distilled, and not always drinkable. For example, one was called "red eye" or "doghouse punch." The recipe differed from ship to ship but the results were the same. Take a gallon of shellac and let the pink liquid come to the top and strain it off. Get some clean sailcloth and strain it a few more times, and then mix it with condensed milk. This would-be poison was claimed by some to be a great pick-up when the spirits were low. It was reported that a quartermaster drank his fill of the punch one day and then lay in the sun to sleep it off. When he woke later it seems that he couldn't talk. The shellac dregs in the punch had dried up in his moustache and beard and he was unable to open his mouth. In 1901, Mrs. Carrie Nation of the Women's Christian Temperance Union in Kansas began her battle against demon rum by smashing up saloons and bars. Her "hatchetations" and violence soon became unpopular, and most mariners were glad that she lived in a landlocked state.

Above: The Steamer *Gate City* of the Savannah Line was bound for Boston on February 8, 1900, when she ran ashore at Moriches, Long Island, N.Y., in dense fog. Life Savers removed 48 persons from the wreck, and the salvors saved part of the cargo but the vessel was a total loss. *Photo from the collection of Paul C. Morris, Nantucket, Massachusetts.* **Below:** On July 11, 1900, the Steamer *Emeline* accidently hit the dock at Newburgh on the Hudson River, New York. Newburgh is 15 miles below Poughkeepsie. The vertical beam engine was caught on dead center and could not be reversed in time to avoid the ship ramming into the dock. This type of slip, while uncommon, was embarrassing to the engineer. The *Emline* was later raised and repaired. *Photo courtesy of the Steamship Historical Society of America.*

Above: A dry-land accident at Camden, Maine, the five-masted schooner *Arthur Seitz* on the ways in 1901. It seems that the cradle slid sideways off the launching ways. The slip gave her a list to starboard and probably scared the people that generally launched aboard. The vessel had to be blocked up and the ways realigned to get her in the water. Old salts say she was hoodooed by christening with flowers instead of breaking a bottle of wine over her bow. This jinxed her from the start and she sailed for only a year. She was wrecked on Skiff Island reef near Muskeget Island, Massachusetts in dense fog on May 25, 1902. *Photo courtesy of Capt. W.J.L. Parker, U.S.C.G. [Ret.]* **Below:** On the afternoon of January 21, 1901, the 422 ton schooner *Joseph Luther* was being towed out of the Kennebec River in Maine. When the tow reached a point just to the windward of Whale's Back Ledge, the hawser parted and she drifted onto the rocks. Life Savers from the Hunnewells Beach Station saved the seven man crew, but the schooner was a total loss. *Photo by Capt. James E. Perkins, courtesy of Jane W. Stevens, Bath, Maine.*

Above: The Joy Line steamer *Old Dominion* ran aground in Long Island Sound near Rye, New York, in dense fog on July 6, 1901. There were 165 passengers asleep at the time of the accident. The vessel ran onto a rocky bottom and punched holes in her hull. The small boat alongside is tending a diver, working under the ship checking her plates. The ship was refloated a month later. **Below:** The ship *Commodore T.H. Allen* with 84,000 cases of kerosene and wax on board cuaght fire outside New York harbor on July 19, 1901 and was very nearly destroyed. New York fireboats and tugs came to her assistance and filled her with water. Much of the upper hamper of the ship was destroyed by the fire, and the hull was later converted to a coal barge. *Photos courtesy of Paul C. Morris, Nantucket, Massachusetts.*

One of the oddest accidents occurred at 10:15 p.m. on June 29, 1901, five miles east of Cape Cod when the only two six-masted schooners in the world collided in fog. The Bath, Maine Daily Times reported that the two ships ''Tried to sail over the same spot on the vast ocean at the same foggy time with costly results.'' **Above:** The view on deck of the *George W. Wells* showing the damage incurred by the collision with the *Eleanor A. Percy.* Forward on the deck is the anchor head of the *Percy* imbedded in the deck timbers of the *Wells.* The port side damage to the huge schooner was extensive. Repairs were estimated to have cost over $20,000. **Below:** The *Eleanor C. Percy* moored at Bath, Maine in July, 1901 minus her jibboom and bowsprit. *Photos courtesy of the Maine Maritime Museum, Bath, Maine.*

Above: On February 2, 1902, the full rigged ship *L. Schepp* of 1,850 tons, bound from Hong Kong to New York City with a general cargo, ran ashore at Point Lookout at Long Beach, New York. The accident report stated: "Ship became unmanageable during a strong westerly gale with a heavy sea and stranded 1,000 yards offshore one mile southwest of Long Beach Life Saving Station." Four days later wrecking crews managed to float the ship. She was towed, half full of water, to New York. Her cargo was badly damaged. *Photo from the collection of Paul C. Morris, Nantucket, Massachusetts.* **Below:** On March 1, 1902, the British steamer *Acara* went ashore on Jones Inlet Bars off Jones Beach, N.Y. The stranding occurred at 2 a.m. during strong southwest winds, with seas running high. Life savers launched surfboats to go to the aid of the crew, but two boats were launched from the wreck with 61 people aboard. Part of the cargo of tea was saved but the hull was a total loss. *Photo courtesy of Mystic Seaport, Mystic, Connecticut.*

Above: The Italian bark *Angela E. Maria* was destroyed by an explosion and fire on July 30, 1903. The ship was being loaded with petroleum and naptha when the accident occurred at the oil docks at Constable Hook at Bayonne, New Jersey. Several of the crew were injured in the fire. The heavily laden ship burned for hours and illuminated the upper bay area of New York. The burning hulk was towed away from the dock and moored in the middle of the bay. Cause of the explosion was reported in the paper as: ''an overpowering desire for baked bologna sausage on the part of the crew, caused the cook to go below and start to bake with the galley stove.'' The explosion occurred when the flames from the stove ignited the naptha fumes. The hull was later converted to a barge. *Photo courtesy of Paul C. Morris, Nantucket, Massachusetts.* **Below:** The Joy Line steamship *Tremont* was destroyed by fire on February 8, 1904, while tied to the pier in New York City. The fire broke out early in the morning and one man was lost in the flames. Two trained lions and a dog which were aboard as cargo were also lost. This type of fire attracts both land and sea firefighters who have unlimited water and the usual result is a sunken hull with a heavily damaged superstructure. The hull was raised by salvagers. *Photo courtesy of the Steamship Historical Society of America.*

Above: The excursion steamer *General Slocum* obviously overloaded with a holiday crowd. These were the days before stringent regulations were enforced on American steamers, sometimes with disastrous results. *Photo courtesy of the Mariners Museum, Newport News, Virginia.*
Below: The burned out wreckage of the *General Slocum* at Hunts Point in New York. On June 15, 1904, the *General Slocum* left the 3rd street dock and headed up the East River for a Sunday school outing with 1,358 passengers, most of whom were children. Fire broke out on board the vessel and could not be controlled. In one of history's worst marine disasters, 1,031 lives were lost that day. Subsequent investigations turned up gross violations of all safety rules and substandard fire fighting equipement on board the excursion vessels of the day. *Photo courtesy Steamship Historical Society of America.*

In the Lutheran Cemetery in Middle Village, Queens, New York, stands a monument in memoriam to those who died on the steamboat *General Slocum* on June 15, 1904. Nearby are buried 958 victims of the disaster. *Photos by Jim Wilson, Steamship Historical Society of America.*

The worst marine disaster in coastal waters around New England happened on June 15, 1904, when the steamer *General Slocum* burned, with the loss of 1031 persons near Hell Gate, New York City. Most of those that died were women and children. The ship was on an annual excursion cruise for the Sunday school classes of St. Marks German Lutheran Church. The disaster was caused by an explosion in the cookstove. The flames spread among the dry wooden beams of the ship covered with many coats of old paint, fanned by a brisk head-on breeze. Soon the entire ship was an inferno, and hysteria spread among the passengers. The panic drove people over the side to escape the flames. Most of these drowned or were crushed under the churning paddle wheels. The captain became alarmed and steered his ship full speed up the river to a remote area off North Brother Island killing scores in his flight.

The aftermath of the tragedy was sickening. The captain was arrested as were many others including crewmen, safety inspectors and company officials. Charges were brought on and leveled at all hands. The only man convicted, however, was Captain William Van Schaick, he received a ten-year sentence for manslaughter, but was pardoned after serving only two years. The claims against the owners of the *General Slocum* arising from the deaths amounted to $1,475,673. This also included $950 for the city of New York for the draping of City Hall. President Theodore Roosevelt personally participated in the firing of many marine inspectors after the *Slocum* disaster. The standards for steamboats were upgraded and improved each year afterward, and then enforced diligently, not only by inspectors but by passengers also. Periodically masters and owners were in court and were fined for laxity in safety rules. Legal compliance became more complex as years passed causing the expense of running vessels to grow with each new rule but boat travel became safer. In later years, older steamboats were retired to the shipbreakers and were not replaced. The burned out hull of the *Slocum* was raised and converted to a coal barge and named *Maryland*. The hull was jinxed and fared a little better. She sank a few times and was raised only to be lost for good when on December 14, 1912 she foundered in a storm off Atlantic City, New Jersey.

Opposite top: The steamer *Monohansett* had an illustrious career. Built in 1862 in New York, of 489 gross tons, she was one of the fastest side wheelers on the coast. She was used during the civil war as a dispatch boat - Richmond to Washington - and often used by President Lincoln. She ran ashore on August 4, 1904, in dense fog at Salem, Massachusetts and became a total loss. *Photo courtesy of the Steamship Historical Society of America.* **Opposite center:** On December 26, 1904, the British steamer *Drumelzier* stranded on Fire Island bar off Long Island, New York, at 3 a.m. during a blinding snow storm. Gusty northeast winds and high seas hampered life saving efforts. The ship rested on the bar for four days and was finally abandoned when high seas endangered the crew. Life Savers rescued the men with lifeboats. The ship was a total loss. *Anderson photo courtesy of the Suffolk Marine Museum, West Sayville, New York.* **Opposite below:** The British steamer *Indus* came ashore at Fire Island, New York, abreast of the lighthouse in dense fog on January 12, 1905. She had sailed from Havana, Cuba, for New York City with a cargo of sugar. Life saving crews from Fire Island and Point of Woods stations made repeated trips through heavy surf to assist the vessel. After much of her cargo was jettisoned, she was refloated on the 15th and steamed to New York. The *Indus* was engaged in the coolie trade and carried more lifeboats than a conventional freighter would normally have. *Photo by Anderson, courtesy of the Suffolk Marine Museum, West Sayville, New York.*

A January blizzard stranded two schooners in Cape Cod Bay in 1905. The *Alice May Davenport* (above) of Bath, Maine and the *Harwood Palmer* (below) of Boston, Mass. Both vessels had anchored to ride out the gale but the anchor chains parted, and the ships went aground. The four-masted *Davenport*, 300 yards off North Dennis, and the five-masted *Palmer*, 200 yards off Yarmouth Beach. The two schooners were caught in winter ice and could not be hauled off until late March. The *Davenport* was hauled off on March 21, 1905 and the *Palmer* was freed on March 24th. *Photo of the Alice May Davenport courtesy of Tales of Cape Cod, Hyannis, Massachusetts. Photo of the Harwood Palmer courtesy of Matthews C. Hallett, Yarmouthport, Massachusetts.*

Above: At Fiddlers Reach on the Kennebec River in Maine, just south of Bath, the *Ranson B. Fuller* went aground early in the morning of August 19, 1905, in thick fog. The steamer was stuck until high tide, later in the day, when she floated off. *Photo by James Perkins, courtesy of Jane Stevens, Bath, Maine.* **Below:** Early in the evening of June 17, 1906, the Italian steamer *Vincenzo Bonanno* stranded on Fire Island, New York, in dense fog, 150 yards from shore. Life Savers rigged the breeches buoy and stood by until wreckers arrived to try to save the ship. The vessel was pulled off ten days later by tugs and towed to New York City. *Photo by Anderson, courtesy of Suffolk Marine Museum, West Sayville, New York.*

The Navy collier *U.S.S. Nero* stranded on Block Island, Rhode Island, in dense fog on August 1, 1906. The ship was out of Norfolk, Virginia, for Newport, Rhode Island, with a cargo of coal. Life Savers from the New Shoreham station aided the steamer crew and radioed for tugs. The vessel was later floated off. *Photo from the collection of Paul C. Morris, Nantucket, Massachusetts.*

A large portion of bulk freight was carried in barges towed by tugs. The traffic around Cape Cod was increasing in 1904. The Lighthouse Board reported seven cases of damage to their light vessels from collisions with barges under tow. The most serious was the Pollock Rip vessel, No. 47, off Chatham which suffered damages when she was hit in dense fog by a barge in tow of a tug owned by the J.B. King Transportation Company of New York. Her false stem was torn off causing her to leak considerably. She was towed to New Bedford and repaired and was back on station within a week. The Shovelful Shoal and Cross Rip ships also suffered minor damages in numerous collisions with barges.

In 1906, nineteen ships sailed from American ports with 257 crewmen and were never heard from again. These included eighteen sailing vessels and one steamer. Early on the morning of March 15, 1907 a heavy gray blanket of fog eneveloped New York harbor and caused a number of accidents. The fog also delayed traffic on land. Two tugs rammed and sunk each other in the harbor. Ashore, two rapid transit trains crashed into each other when the motormen missed the signals in the morning mist. The fog lifted in the afternoon.

On February 11, 1908, ice clogged the New York harbor and waterways. In the outer bays, ocean liners had to wait for clear water. Ferry service was curtailed because of the heavy ice chunks in the inner harbor. Barge traffic was halted because many were sunk or damaged. A fishing sloop was crushed and her decks awash when the vessel drifted past Sandy Hook, and the Tarrytown and Rockland Lake lighthouses were surrounded by piles of ice, making it difficult for the light Keepers to get ashore. The New York Society for the Prevention of Cruelty to Animals spread ashes over the icy streets of New York so that horses would not fall and break their legs on the slippery roads.

Left: Ships sometimes become legends. The *City of Bangor* was one of these. In June of 1894 she began steaming on the Penobscot River in Maine and ran for over twenty years. She had some adventures along the way. On September 28, 1902, she struck on Monhegan Island in thick fog and was run on the beach at Lobster Cove to prevent her sinking. **Above:** in June, 1906, she was in collision with her sister ship the *City of Rockland* and suffered the loss of her bow. *Photos courtesy of Frank Claes.* There was a fire aboard the *City of Bangor* on June 18, 1913 in Boston. **Below:** She finished her days at Federal Wharf in East Boston when she sank on December 27, 1933, beside the four-masted schooner *Snetind*. She went out of documentation in 1935. *Photo by R. Loren Graham courtesy of the Steamship Historical Society of America.*

On October 13, 1906 an autumn fog was the cause of a collision between the Hudson River steamboats *Adirondack* and the *Saratoga*. The *Saratoga* suffered the most damage. The crash tore away the outboard housing of the paddle wheel and caused the port boiler to roll overboard. One man was lost off each vessel. The *Saratoga* sank near Barrytown. She was subsequently raised and repaired and ran on the river until 1910. An old superstition about a steamboat with a name beginning with the letter S came true for the *Saratoga*. The ship was plagued with bad luck. *Photo courtesy of the Steamship Historical Society of America.*

Late on the night of February 11, 1907 in Block Island sound with the air temperature at three degrees F, the schooner *Harry Knowlton*, sailing with a fair wind and all sails set, rammed the passenger steamer *Larchmont* with 150 passengers and a crew of 35. The schooner struck the steamer amidships forward of the paddlewheel. Both vessels suffered fatal damage. The schooner with a load of coal grounded near Block Island and was a total loss. Her crew of seven landed in the ship's boat. The *Larchmont* sank in twelve minutes, carrying half of the people aboard her down as she sank. The other half nearly all froze to death in the open lifeboats. The boats came ashore on Block Island the next day, and of the nearly 200 persons on board the steamer only 20 survived, and three of those died later. One of the deciding factors of the high death rate was the lack of time to fire rockets or other distress signals to bring help from shore. It was a clear night and many could have been saved. The accident occurred only three or four miles off shore from the Life Saving crews on Block Island.

In New York City, the Society for Suppression of Unnecessary Noises charged two Moran Company tugboat captains with disturbing the peace by tooting their whistles along the North River. Three long and two short blasts were heard at approximately 5:40 a.m. on April 7, 1907. It seems that this was the "Scow Call," used to wake up the crew of the barge to hook up to the tow. At the hearing the tugboat men agreed as how they might have blown the whistle but only when necessary. ". . . we have to beat the tide, Government regulations control the traffic, got to blow the whistle, etc. . . . " The captains presented their case while the ladies of the Society for Unnecessary Noise claimed that the tooting was done in order to call the scowmen out of the nearby saloons, and that the tugboat men would also sometimes beam their searchlights and toot their whistles in front of the plush neighborhood homes along the North River. After a few more charges by the women, the men of the Board of New York Steamboat Inspectors declared the case closed and said that they would render a decision at a later date. A careful search of the records failed to turn up the decision.

Above: The passenger steamer *Larchmont* was sunk on the night of February 11, 1907, in Block Island sound off Rhode Island, in collision with the schooner *Harry Knowlton.* Of the 200 plus persons aboard the *Larchmont,* only 17 survived to tell of the ordeal. The steamer sank in 12 minutes, after only half of the people on board had managed to get aboard life boats and rafts. The high winds and zero degree temperatures took a high toll. *Photo - authors collection.* **Below:** The wreckage of the schooner *Harry Knowlton* came ashore on Quonochontaug beach on the south shore of Rhode Island and was a total wreck. The *Larchmont/Knowlton* disaster is considered by marine historians to be one of the major casualties of the decade. *Photo courtesy of the Mariners Museum, Newport News, Virginia.*

Above: The largest five-masted schooner built was almost destroyed in an $100,000 fire that ravaged the East Boston waterfront on August 26-27, 1907. The fire burned the rigging, cabins, deck and cargo of the *Jane Palmer* before firemen put out the flames. The vessel was repaired and went back to sea. *Photo courtesy of Frank Claes, Orland, Maine.* **Below:** On February 2, 1908 a southeast gale cast the British bark *Puritan* ashore on Long Island, N.Y., near Bellport. Life Savers from the Bellport station assisted the crew of 16 ashore via lifeboat. The Master and Mate remained on board. The ship was aground until wreckers refloated her on February 28th. *Photo courtesy of Capt. W.J. Lewis Parker, U.S.C.G.* [*Ret.*]

Above: The German ship *Peter Rickmers* bound from Perth Amboy, N.J. to Rangoon, Burma, was wrecked near Jones Beach, Long Island, N.Y., on April 30, 1908, during thick weather and an easterly gale. The ship was heavily laden with a cargo of 125,000 cases of crude oil and kerosene. Life Savers from the Short Beach Station landed the crew of 33, and wreckers were called to save the vessel. **Below:** A few days later the storm had finished the ship, and she broke up and was a total loss. *Photos from the collection of Paul C. Morris, Nantucket, Massachusetts.*

Above: Divers are down on the steamer *Boothbay* in Bath, Maine. On June 1, 1908, she caught her port guard on the wharf during a night tide, listed to starboard, and had water flow into her ports. It took three weeks to raise her, and then she had to be rebuilt. The steamer *Camden* is in the background. *Photo courtesy of the Bath Marine Museum, Bath, Maine.* **Below:** On April 9, 1908, at Shinnecock, Long Island, N.Y., the schooner *George P. Hudson* stranded at 2 a.m. in thick weather one mile east of the Shinnecock Life Saving Station. The vessel was discovered by the east patrol at 4:45 a.m., and life savers set up the breeches buoy. The Master landed and made communications with wreckers. That afternoon the tug *I.J. Merritt* arrived and began salvage. The schooner was refloated on the 19th. *Photo courtesy of Capt. W.J. Parker, U.S.C.G. [Ret.]*

On July 19, 1904, the steamer *H.M. Whitney* ran into Relief light-vessel No. 58 while the latter was on station at Pollock Rip. The damage to the light-vessel was extensive but entirely above water. There was no danger and the light-vessel remained on station until July 24th when the regular light-vessel returned. The steamer *H.M. Whitney* was sunk in a collision in Boston harbor in 1892. (Page 22) and in 1908 had two accidents at Hell Gate near New York City. On May 23, 1908, her steering gear broke, and she went on the rocks at Ward's Island. The 271-foot vessel was raised, pumped out, and repaired. **Above:** On November 5, 1908, the ship was headed out of New York for Boston when she swerved to avoid a collision with a barge which had women and children on board. She went on the rocks at Ward's Island and sank by the stern. Her crew barely escaped when the vessel went down. *Photo courtesy of the Mariners Museum, Newport News, Virginia.* **Below:** She was salvaged by the Merritt-Chapman Company and went back in service on the New York - Boston run. *Photo courtesy of Mystic Seaport, Mystic, Connecticut.*

The Italian liner *Florida* lost her bow in a collision with the British steamer *Republic* 26 miles southwest of Nantucket Island. The *Republic* sank with the loss of six lives. This was the first marine disaster where the wireless radio played an important part in the rescue of persons at sea on January 23, 1909. *Photo courtesy of the Peabody Museum of Salem.*

On January 23, 1909 in dense fog 26 miles southwest of Nantucket Island the Italian liner *Florida* sliced into the side of the British steamer *Republic* ripping open the hull to the cold Atlantic. Six lives were lost but, more important, it was the first use of the new radio wireless to call for help. The collision bulkhead on the *Florida* held up but she lost thirty feet of her bow. The *Republic* was a doomed ship and the radio operator Jack Binns became famous as he stood by his radio key tapping out the S O S messages to bring aid to the sinking vessel. The steamer *Baltic* arrived on scene and rescued 1,650 passengers from the two vessels - a vast undertaking using small boats at sea. The *Republic* was sinking and the Revenue cutter *Gresham* took her in tow for shoal water but she sank before they could save her. All hands except the six killed in the initial collision were saved. Jack Binns had transmitted more than 200 messages during the ordeal. He was lauded around the world. Unique was the magic of the new radio and its ability to save lives at sea in a disaster. Binns' messages brought nearby ships to the scene of the accident quickly.

Ships are wrecked and many times the eyewitnesses are not able to give the reasons why or are not able to be understood. The sailors vernacular bodes ill for factual information. Some of the words and phrases used aboard ship were reported in an early edition of the New York Times, relating to a report in a court of inquiry by a nautical witness: "We was going along all fluking when the wind drawed ahead. We trimmed sail, and in fore and mizzen tor'garns'l, when a bit of sea makin' of her yaw. 'Mind yer luff, you soger' sings out the old man, an' as he says this, one of the jib guys parted and sprung the boom, for ours were swinging booms and had the for'd guy and the after guy fitted in one, with a cuckold's neck around the boom end. Are yer followin' of me sir?" This was all very clear to his shipmates but to investigators on shore, it left them at sea.

Above: Late at night on February 19, 1909, the freight steamer *John H. Starin* was battling an easterly gale in Long Island Sound. The ship, built as a revenue cutter in 1865, was carrying a heavy load of freight. Some of the seams opened up and she began to take on water rapidly and the crewmen were working at the pumps steadily. The storm and leaks got worse and the stokers in the engine room were working in water up to their knees. The pilot had just spotted the lights on Steeplechase Island breakwater when the steamer lost her way and went on the rocks. Some of the cargo was recovered but the ship was a total loss. *Photo above courtesy of the Mariners Museum, Newport News, Virgina.* **Below:** The five-masted schooner *William C. Carnegie* was wrecked at East Moriches, Long Island, New York, on May 1, 1909, in a northeast gale. Twenty-foot seas prevented life savers from effecting a lifeboat rescue from shore. The crew of the schooner cleared a long boat and rowed off shore to await rescue by the cutter *Mohawk*. The vessel was loaded with 4,400 tons of coal. The ship and cargo was a total loss. *Photo courtesy of Capt. W.J. Lewis Parker, U.S.C.G. [Ret.]*

Above: The *Alice E. Clark,* a 1,621 G.T. coal schooner was sailing up in Penobscot Bay early in the evening of July 1, 1909, when she ran onto Coombs Ledge and sank. Salvage experts spent a few thousand dollars trying to save her, but in December a heavy gale struck and the vessel broke into pieces and disappeared. *Photo from the collection of Paul C. Morris, Nantucket, Massachusetts.* **Below:** The granite lighters *Benjamin Franklin* and *Potomac* were driven ashore at Sandwich, Massachusetts, in a northeast gale on November 9, 1909. The two lighters with 23 crewmen on board were part of a group of vessels engaged in laying a breakwater for the new Cape Cod Canal. The vessels were a total loss. *Photo by Small, courtesy of the Bourne Historical Society.*

CHAPTER FIVE

The schooner *Daylight* with a cargo of 1,000 tons of coal sank shortly before noon on January 18, 1910, in Lower Bay, New York after she struck a partially sunken mud dumper scow. The Captain and crew were saved and the schooner was refloated on March 28th. *Photo from the collection of Paul C. Morris, Nantucket, Massachusetts.*

In 1910, the use of the wireless-radio dominated the shipping news. Proposals to centralize wireless operations and Government controls to expedite service were reviewed at great lengths. In January 1910, the first weather information was flashed to the sea from the naval wireless station at Newport, Rhode Island. The weather messages were picked up by the Nantucket Shoals lightship and relayed to other ships in the vicinity who in turn passed them along to those farther out at sea. This, in effect, was the beginning of warnings to ships at sea about oncoming storms.

About this time Henry Ford was mass-producing model T Fords. There were other more expensive autos with familiar names like Simplex, Packard, Maxwell and Cadillac, but the reason for the popularity of the Ford was its simplicity. It was not too expensive for the average American. In May of 1910 the price for a four cylinder, 20 H.P., five passenger sedan completely equipped with top, speedometer, windshield, gas lamps, generators, oil lamps, horn, tools and tire repair kit was $950. By 1917, it had dropped to $650, and Henry Ford said that you could have any color you wanted as long as it was black. The expanding popularity of the automobile brought demands for a new network of highways to be built all over the country, so that America could take advantage of this new freedom in travel and go anywhere in a hurry at 25 to 30 miles per hour. The development of the automobile was to be one cause of the future demise of the coastal passenger steamers.

The 1910 census reported that ninety million people made up the population of the United States as 700,000 more immigrants arrived in New York to seek a new life in the land of opportunity. In May, 1910, Halley's Comet was visible in the night skies. In June, 1910, the *Shenendoah,* the largest square rigged ship, built at Bath, Maine, was cut down to a coal barge. Built in 1890, of 3,154 tons, she was 300' long and carried about two acres of sails. Captain Jim Murphy claimed she sailed like a knock-about sloop. In her twenty-year career she sailed around the world and around Cape Horn several times. Stripped of mast and sail she suffered the ultimate humiliation until she was lost off Long Island in 1918. These were the twilight years for the sailing ship.

65

Above: The steamer *William Fletcher* which ran between the Battery and Ellis Island, New York, hit a spar and sprang a leak and then sank off Governors Island on March 23, 1910. **Below:** Two Merrit Chapman Company derrick barges lifted the vessel off the bottom. *Photos courtesy of Mystic Seaport, Mystic, Connecticut.*

Above: The German steamer *Prinzess Irene* carrying 1,725 passengers stranded on the south beach of Long Island, New York, on April 6, 1911, at 4 a.m. in dense fog. She was spotted by the east patrol from the Lone Hill Life Saving Station. Men from this station boarded the grounded vessel by lifeboat and then sent messages to the owners, revenue cutters and wreckers. The seas were calm, and there was no danger. The next afternoon all of the passengers were transferred by lifeboat to the *S.S. Prinz Freidrich Wilhelm*. On April 9, after passengers and cargo were removed, the steamer was pulled off the beach and escorted to New York City. *Photo by Anderson, courtesy of the Suffolk Marine Museum, West Sayville, New York.* **Below:** On May 17, 1910 just after unloading a cargo of gasoline onto a barge in Provincetown harbor, a crewman lit a cabin light and the schooner *Estelle S. Nunan* went up in flames. The crewman was thrown into the harbor but was saved. The vessel was a total loss. *Photo courtesy of Cyril Patrick, Provincetown, Massachusetts.*

Above: The men in the small boat are tending a diver down on the Canadian schooner *Garfield White* which sank off Coney Island on July 5, 1910. She had sprung a leak while on her way to Canada with a load of coal. The crew fought for 24 hours to save the vessel, but the ship leaked faster than they could pump her out. They abandoned the ship and made their way ashore in the ship's boat. **Below:** The steamer *Penobscot* went aground on the night of June 11, 1911, in the Hudson River during an extra high tide. The ship was stuck at Stockport Flats for 26 days. It was necessary to dredge around her and with the help of several steam derricks and a dozen tugboats the vessel was refloated. In 1918 the old hull was converted to a five-masted schooner and named the *Mohawk* and sailed for less than a year and went missing. *Photos from the collection of Paul C. Morris, Nantucket, Massachusetts.*

Wreckers pick over the remains of the Barge *Pine Forest*, one of three barges wrecked in a storm off Cape Cod on January 10, 1911. The wood salvaged from the wreckage was used mostly as firewood but some of the larger beams were used in construction of houses. *Photo courtesy of Tales of Cape Cod, Inc., Barnstable, Massachusetts.*

On January 10, 1911, the tug *Lykens* and three coal barges - The *Trevorton,* the *Corbin,* and the *Pine Forest* - headed north off Cape Cod and hit a gale. The tug lost the tow late at night. Sixty m.p.h. winds prevailed, and the barges were wrecked. No trace of the *Trevorton* or the *Corbin* was ever found, and speculation was that they collided and sank. The *Pine Forest* was driven in the gale winds onto the Peaked Hill Bars in Provincetown, where she grounded on the outer bar. The tug tried to hook up to the barge again but shoal water and high winds prevented her from doing so. The crew of five tried to launch their small boat, but it capsized in the mountainous seas, and all five crewmen were lost. The *Pine Forest* later broke up, and pieces came ashore in the surf. There were numerous cases of barges being abandoned by tugs at sea in rough weather, leaving the vessels to anchor and the crews to pray while the tug went into a safe harbor nearby to wait out the weather. When the storm abated and the tug returned to the tow she usually found the barges wrecked or sunk.

The United States Life Saving Service carried out their duties from August to May each year, giving the surfmen two months off every summer. There was some criticism in June, 1911, for closing the stations for two months in the interest of economy. Many mariners protested the closings and, with tongue in cheek, proposed to close fire departments on shore during the same time because furnaces are then turned off in private homes. Therefore, they reasoned, there would be no domestic fires. The records showed some appalling marine disasters during the summer months, with numerous fatal results. But Life Savers still had their summers off - until 1917, after the formation of the Coast Guard.

In January, 1912, the British steamer Birchfield arrived in New York harbor with her coal bunkers ablaze. The fire had started at sea. Crewmen could not bring it under control and the ship became like an oven. It was so hot below decks that the cook could not stand the heat in the galley. He came up on deck and literally cooked flapjacks on the iron deck for the crews' breakfast, while the New York firemen extinguished the smoldering coal.

On October 7, 1911, the three-masted schooner *Frederick Roessner* ran up on the breakwater near Peacock Point in Matinicock, Long Island, New York. A storm with high winds and rain caused the grounding on the rocks and stove a hole in the bottom of the vessel. The schooner had a cargo of stone which was unloaded. She was hauled off on the 16th and towed to New York City for repairs. *Photo from the collection of Paul C. Morris, Nantucket, Massachusetts.*

Early in the morning of July 7, 1912, the Fall River liner *Commonwealth* (page 105)rammed into the stern of the *U.S.S. New Hampshire* in dense fog in Newport Harbor, Rhode Island. The collision ripped some steel plates on the battleship. The damage to the *Commonwealth* was a mangled bow. One man aboard the Navy ship was injured. There were no injuries on the passenger liner, but the damage laid the huge steamer up for about a month during the busy summer season. *Photo courtesy of the Steamship Historical Society of America.*

Above: The Maine Central steamboat *Norumbega* aground at Clarks Point near Northeast Harbor on August 13, 1912. This was an odd type of accident. Firemen had banked the fires anticipating a short run across the harbor. A short delay in departure caused the vessel to run out of steam halfway to her destination. She ran aground in dense fog on a high tide but was pulled off with little damage. *Photo courtesy of Allie Ryan, South Brooksville, Maine.* **Below:** On October 10, 1912, a boiler explosion on the oil tanker *Dunholme* caused a conflagration at the Standard Oil Company oil docks on Constable Hook in Bayonne, N.J. Flames from the fully laden tanker spread quickly to four other ships at the docks. Two of the ships were saved but two others, the *Concordia* below and the *Hohenzollern,* were lost to the fire. The flames created what was referred to as a brilliant spectacle, but it cost the lives of three men. *Photo from the collection of Paul C. Morris, Nantucket, Massachusetts.*

Above: The barkentine *Antioch* battling stormy weather south of New York City went aground near the Squan Beach, New Jersey Life Saving Station on March 27, 1913, at 4:30 a.m. Life savers rescued the crew of 10 with the breeches buoy. *Photo from the collection of Paul C. Morris, Nantucket, Massachusetts.* **Below:** The *Iroquois,* formerly the *Kennebec,* ran aground on the Hudson River in a night fog at Cementon, New York, on April 20, 1914. The *C.W. Morse* tied on to the grounded vessel and tried to pull her off, but the hawser broke. The *Iroquois* was stuck on the bank for a week before she was pulled off by the wrecking steamer *Champion. Photo courtesy of Allie Ryan, South Brooksville, Maine.*

Above: The work of rescue attracted a large crowd on February 7, 1914 when the British steamer *Queen Louise* stranded near Squan Beach, New Jersey in dense fog. There is a movie camera located behind the breeches buoy crotch. Perhaps the rescue appeared in the newsreels. The vessel was refloated three days later with no damage. *Photo courtesy of the Mariners Museum, Newport News, Virginia.* **Below:** One of the giant coal schooners was wrecked in a storm on Tuckernuck Shoal off Nantucket Island, Massachusetts on December 5, 1914. The *Alice M. Lawrence,* bound ''light'' from Portland, Maine to Norfolk, Virginia, ran up on the wreck of the schooner *French Van Gilder,* which was loaded with granite paving blocks and was wrecked on the same spot 29 years earlier. Salvors had hoped to save the 305-foot schooner, one of the nine six-masters on the east coast, but the vessel broke her back on top of the other wreck. *Photo courtesy of Charlie Sayle, Nantucket, Massachusetts.*

The 66,000 ton *Titanic* is shown leaving Europe on her maiden voyage to the United States in April, 1912. The huge ship struck an iceberg and went to the bottom taking over 1500 people to their deaths. The *Titanic* carried lifeboats for only half of her passengers and her loss is considered the greatest tragedy in the history of ocean travel. *Photo courtesy of the Titanic Historical Society, Inc., Indian Orchard, Massachusetts.*

On April 14th, the brand new White Star liner *Titanic* was steaming along in the North Atlantic at 22½ knots on her maiden voyage to America. Just before midnight the big four-stacker rammed into an iceberg at 41°46'N and 50°14'W, about 400 miles south east of Newfoundland, tearing a huge hole in her hull. The big ship was doomed. She sank in a little over two hours. 1503 persons were lost, and only 703 people survived in lifeboats. The aftermath of the sinking - which cost some noted Americans their lives - resulted in new and demanding regulations on ocean liners. A serious lifeboat shortage ensued when liners in ports all over the world tried to bring up the number of their lifeboats to the capacity of passengers on board. Following the *Titanic* disaster the Marconi company was unable to provide all of the radio operators for the ships that now demanded them. New schools were operated to train more wireless men.

The territory of Arizona had become a state in 1912, thus completing the physical United States from the Atlantic to the Pacific. In this same period of time, in their battle against liquor, the Women's Christian Temperence Union called on New York Governor Dix to launch a new ship with water instead of wine. In 1913, the United States Post Office began parcel post service. America was in a business recession in 1913-14, but was soon bailed out with the huge orders for war materials from Europe. The January and February gales in the North Atlantic caused a major disruption of passenger service. Many steamers recorded rough voyages, and the liner *Mauretania* reported hitting a giant wave an a trip across the North Atlantic.

On May 29, 1914, the *Empress of Ireland*, a British steamer, left Quebec bound for Liverpool, England. The vessel was stopped by dense fog off Father Point in the St. Lawrence River when she was struck amidships by the Norwegian collier *Storstad*. Several persons were killed in the initial impact. A total of 1024 people died in the accident. In the summer of 1914 two new ship canals were opened: On July 29, the Cape Cod Canal in Massachusetts, and on August 15 the Panama Canal, which rerouted traffic from around Cape Horn, South America. In 1914 the war began in Europe, and President Wilson proclaimed United States' neutrality.

Above: The tug *Watuppa* towing a barge through the newly opened Cape Cod Canal struck a washout near Bournedale on January 30, 1915, and sank with her bow on the canal bank. The tug was salvaged by a wrecking tug from Boston and was in service to the 1940's. *Photo by Small courtesy of the Bourne Historical Society.* **Below:** The British bark *Hugomont* stranded on Fire Island, New York, on February 6, 1915. The ship was from London to New York with a cargo of chalk. The Coast Guard set up the breeches buoy and removed the crew of 20, while 7 crewmen remained aboard. The wreckers arrived and, after unloading a third of her cargo, they refloated the bark on the 19th and towed her to New York City. *Photo courtesy of Capt. W.J.L. Parker, U.S.C.G. [Ret.]*

Above: An early morning fog caused the collision between the steamers *Pemaquid* and *J.T. Morse* on September 8, 1915, at the western entrance to Deer Island thoroughfare near Stonington, Maine. Captain Addison W. Shute managed to bring his vessel into a wharf on Moose Island before it sank to her freight deck. Passengers and cargo were removed and the ship made tight and pumped out. She then went to Boston under her own power for repairs. *Photo courtesy of the Steamship Historical Society of America.* **Below:** The Long Island Sound steamer *Isabel* sunk at Shippan Point just south of Stamford, Connecticut on September 28, 1915. Some of her cargo is stacked on deck as another steamer pulls alongside. Most of her cargo was recovered but the ship was lost. *Photo courtesy of Paul C. Morris, Nantucket, Massachusetts.*

Above: The three-masted schooner *William L. Elkins* was caught on a reef off Cape Elizabeth, Maine during a northeast gale on December 6, 1915. The Coast Guard Cutter *Ossipee* arrived on the scene and removed the crew of six. The vessel was a total loss. *Photo courtesy of Robert Beattie.* **Below:** Two barges were wrecked and four men drowned when a northeast gale hit the Massachusetts coast on March 4, 1916. Off North Scituate two coal barges, the *Kohinoor* and *The Ashland*, parted their tow lines and were smashed to pieces on the ledges near Minots Ledge lighthouse. The deck house of the barge *Ashland* was still afloat with five men clinging to it when the Coast Guard fired a shot line to the floating wreckage and then helped the survivors ashore.

The Norwegian bark *Clan Galbraith* went aground near Shinnecock Inlet, Long Island, New York, on July 22, 1916. The iron hulled vessel suffered little damage and lay on the sand for about two weeks. On August 4th tugs from the Merritt Chapman Company refloated the huge square rigger. The ship was later sunk by a German U-boat. *Photo courtesy of Paul C. Morris, Nantucket, Massachusetts.*

In February, 1915, there were sixty-six German and Austrian vessels interned in American ports, including the *Vaterland,* the 54,000-ton German giant. In May, a German submarine sank the Cunard liner, *Lusitania,* as she was completing a transatlantic crossing near England. Twelve hundred people died, including 128 United States citizens. This brought the war closer to America. In Chicago, another excursion vessel disaster occurred on July 24th when the top heavy steamer *Eastland* capsized at dockside, which caused more than 800 people to drown. In New York harbor, bombs were being planted by saboteurs on ships carrying war materials to Europe. Many ships went missing.

In the winter of 1915-16 storms delayed many ships in New York harbor and drove others at sea into Bermuda and Nova Scotia to refill their coal bunkers. The port of Bermuda ran out of coal causing many ships to be stranded with cargoes of war materials bound for Europe. In a dense fog the Fire Island lightship was rammed at 4 o'clock in the morning of May 9, 1916, by the British liner *Philadelphian.* The lightship was heavily damaged but did not sink. The *Philadelphian* towed the lightship into New York harbor. On Sunday, July 30, 1916 at 3 a.m. a huge explosion rocked New York City as some war munitions were blown up on a New Jersey pier. The blast was felt ninety miles away, with the explosion wrecking a seven million dollar storage plant and killing many people.

The German submarine menace grew worse and some American ships became casualties. When this occurred, the German Government would apologize to the United States. Some high American officials were quoted as saying: ''We are in the war now! The only thing is that we are not fighting back!'' In March of 1917, German submarines sank four American ships with the loss of 36 persons. War was declared on April 6, 1917, Good Friday. Cargo ships became scarcer. Hulls for war goods and the coal to run them was in short supply. Almost anything that would float was pressed into service. Old wooden schooners, now an anacronism, were again carrying cargoes along the coasts and across the oceans. Canadian ships were allowed to engage in United States coastal commerce to help relieve port congestion.

Above: The steamer *Bay State*, sister ship to the *Portland* - lost with all hands in the great gale of 1898 - was wrecked on Holycomb Ledge, on Cape Elizabeth, Maine, in dense fog on September 23, 1916. The sea was calm and all passengers and crewmen were taken off safely. **Below:** The heavy pounding of storm seas soon demolished the grounded vessel. *Photos courtesy of the Peabody Museum of Salem.*

Above: The four-masted schooner *Dustin G. Cressy* was rammed by the steamer *Valeria* in New York lower bay on February 19, 1917. She was struck on the starboard side about amidships and she rolled over on her beam ends. **Below:** A Merritt Chapman derrick righted her and the vessel was repaired and went back to sea. *Photos courtesy of Paul C. Morris, Nantucket, Massachusetts.*

On August 1, 1917, the hospital ship *Letitia* was wrecked in dense fog just inside Chebucto Head outside Halifax, Nova Scotia. The ship was carrying 546 wounded soldiers back from the war in Europe and all were saved. the pilot had just taken the con to bring her into Halifax and he signaled for more speed. Ten minutes later the ship piled up on the rocks and was a total wreck. *Photo courtesy of the Public Archives of Nova Scotia.*

On December 6, 1917 the French freighter *Mont Blanc,* with a load of munitions, collided with the Norwegian steamship, *Imo,* in Halifax Harbor. A fire broke out aboard the *Mont Blanc* as a result of the collision and shortly afterward she exploded, nearly obliterating the city of Halifax. The blast caused a loss of thirty-five million dollars in property damage and killed over 1,600 persons and injured 9,000 more. Relief was sent from St. John, New Brunswick, via rail but a blizzard held up rescue efforts. Other trains, with hundreds of injured being carried away from the city, were stalled in the snow. The city was isolated by the storm, making further rescue of persons trapped in wrecked buildings more difficult. War veterans called the scene at Halifax worse than a battlefield.

In 1918, additional efforts were underway to relieve the shortage of ships. The United States shipping board included concrete ships in their plans for an emergency fleet. Trial runs had been completed with the first concrete ship. Built on the west coast, she was named *Faith*. The cost of one year of war was set at nine billion dollars, of which almost five billion was in loans to our Allies. Drastic changes were ordered in the lifeboat regulations because of war losses. All vessels entering the war zones were required to provide lifeboat space for all on board.

Early in the war, Allied forces were just holding their own against the advancing German Army. The Russians had been beaten, and many German troops were transferred from the eastern front to the western front in France. After the United States entered the war, the build-up of forces in France drove the Germans back, and the Allies finally won the war. On November 11, 1918, the Armistice was signed and the war was over. In 1919 the first transatlantic flight was accomplished by an American Naval plane, the NC-4 flew via Newfoundland and the Azores.

A wartime measure with lingering effects was the Volstead Act, or Prohibition. Bread from grain was more necessary than whiskey and by January, 1919, the necessary thirty-six states had approved the 18th amendment to the United States Constitution. Times changed abruptly and prohibition brought on the speakeasy, the bootlegger, the rumrunners and the roaring '20s.

Above: The Norwegian steamer *Imo*, beached and gutted. On December 6, 1917 the *Imo* was in collision with the French munitions freighter *Mont Blanc* in Halifax, Nova Scotia harbor. A fire broke out on the freighter and she exploded, turning the port into a mass of ruins. **Below:** There was thirty-five million dollars in property damage at Halifax. Sixteen hundred people were killed and nine thousand injured. *Photos courtesy of the Public Archives of Nova Scotia.*

Above: The *H.F. Dimock* had a long career on the Boston to New York run. However, her accidents were many and varied. In 1892 she rammed and sank the Vanderbuilt yacht *Alva* in Pollock Rip Slue off Cape Cod. On June 16, 1902, the *Dimock* was in collision with the New York excursion steamer *Cygnus* in New York harbor. Cause of the accident was listed as a mixup in signals. In 1909 she rammed and sank the steamer *Horatio Hall,* again in Pollock Rip Slue off Cape Cod. On November 18, 1912, a fire of unknown origin broke out in the forward hold of the vessel at Pier 15, in New York City. The steel hull of the steamer was not damaged, but a large part of the superstructure was destroyed before New York firefighters brought the blaze under control. The vessel was rebuilt. On December 26, 1917 the *Dimock* was heading up the East River in New York and she grounded near the abutment of the Williamsburg Bridge. The ship sank but was raised on January 4, 1918 and brought to the pier as shown in the photograph above. She was repaired and went back on the run. The ship continued to sail until 1933 when she was abandoned and soon after was scrapped. *Photo from the collection of Frank E. Claes, Orland, Maine.* **Below:** The steamer *San Jose* rammed the four-masted schooner *Governor Powers* on September 11, 1918, near Half Moon Shoal in Nantucket sound. The vessel rolled over on her beam ends and was towed to shoal waters for salvage but proved to be a total loss. There was $50,000 damage to the steamer. *Photo by Bob Beattie.*

Above: On February 28, 1919 the steamer *Aquitania* coming up New York harbor collided with the British freighter *Lord Dufferin*. Damage to the freighter was extensive and resulted in lengthy lawsuits. The ship lost about forty feet of her stern. The hull was immediately beached. She was refloated on March 21st. *Photo courtesy of the Mariners Museum, Newport News, Virginia.* **Below:** The palatial yacht *United States* ran aground on a rock ledge in Padanaram harbor in South Dartmouth, Massachusetts, on August 21, 1919. Wrecking crews from the T.A. Scott Company spent a couple of weeks getting her on an even keel and then pulling her off the rocks. She was towed to a shipyard for repairs. *Photo by Robert Beattie.*

Above: The steamer *Nantucket,* built in 1886 ran year-round service to the islands for 26 years. She was sold to a New York shipping firm and her name was changed to *Point Comfort.* On the night of September 17, 1919 while headed up the river, the crew lost their bearings in dense fog and ran the steamer on the rocks of the northern end of Esopus Island near Hyde Park. There were no injuries, and the crew put over a lifeboat and rowed to Hyde Park. The *Point Comfort* never sailed again. She slowly disintegrated. *Photo from the collection of Paul C. Morris, Nantucket, Massachusetts.* **Below:** In the early 1920's the facade of the T.A. Scott Company shipyard storehouse in New London, Connecticut displayed quarterboards from numerous vessels wrecked up and down the coast of New England. The grim list resembled an obituary. Perhaps as a warning to mariners. *Photo by Bob Beattie.*

CHAPTER SIX

The decline and demise of the large wooden schooner from the maritime trades is illustrated by this group of ships lying idle in Mill Cove at Boothbay Harbor in the late 1930's. *Photo courtesy of Bill Fuller, Jr.*

When World War I ended the commercial shipping business dwindled, and the old wooden sailing vessels started to slip into oblivion. Many of the old four-masted schooners still carried bulk freight cheaper than the steamers, but at the whim of wind and weather. It was difficult to compete with scheduled arrivals and departures maintained by the steam vessels. For every schooner sailing there were ten more laid up in harbors and ports up and down the Atlantic coast from Maine to Florida. Some of the three and four-masters continued to sail into the 1930's, but several of the old hulls were cut down to barges, tethered behind steam tugs in lots of three or four in a tow. A large number of them were consigned to the ship graveyards. It is indeed unfortunate that not one of these work-horses of the past was ever preserved for posterity. Some of the tall wooden masts were reborn as flagpoles in small town squares, while the ships' planking, impregnated with salt from the years at sea made rugged foundations for Cape Cod cottages in many New England towns. One inventive use for an old wooden hull was to sink it in shoal waters outside harbors for use as a breakwater or sometimes inside the harbor as a wharf.

Above: The *Cora F. Cressy* on launching day in Bath, Maine, 1902, a handsome five-master. She had a long career sailing over 25 years in the coal trade. *Photo courtesy of Paul C. Morris, Nantucket, Massachusetts.* **Below:** She ended up as a breakwater for a lobster pound in Medomak, Maine. *Photo by William P. Quinn.*

Above: In 1932, the four-masted schooners *Hesper* and *Luther Little* were hauled into Wiscasset, Maine, and laid up alongside a wharf. They have never moved since then and have become a top tourist attraction as they rot away in the elements. *Photo courtesy of Bill Fuller, Jr.* **Below:** In 1977 the deterioration is gaining on the old hulls and soon they will be like their sister ships, things of the past. *Photo by William P. Quinn.*

Above: A contrasting view showing the steep angle of the headgear of the schooner *Northland*. The jibboom end was usually some fifty feet above water and, in schooner-steamer collisions, the pilot house of the steamer took the worst damage. A unique case occurred on the night of May 10, 1907, late at night in Nantucket Sound. The four-masted schooner *Sagamore*, sailing west was in collision with the Norwegian steamer *Edda*. The bowsprit of the schooner swept over the bridge of the steamer and picked up her captain and carried him out over the water where he watched his ship steaming off without him. He crawled back along the jibboom and made his way to the stern of the sailing vessel and informed the captain of his predicament. The *Sagamore* started to sink as a result of the collision, and all hands went into the yawl boat and rowed ashore to Martha's Vineyard. The steamer had run aground lightly and damage was slight, but the schooner sank in the sound with only her topmasts showing. **Below:** Broken headgear was a normal occurrence with schooners. The *Lavinia M. Snow* is shown after a minor collision. *Photos from the marine collection of Frank E. Claes, Orland, Maine.*

Above: The *Thomas W. Lawson,* the one and only seven-masted schooner. Built in Quincy, Massachusetts in 1902 she was unique in that she had a steel hull and masts. She measured 5,218 gross tons. She could carry a prodigious amount of coal, some 11,000 tons fully loaded. To drive her over the ocean, she spread 44,000 square feet of sail and drew 29½ feet of water. This caused her to go aground many times. She was known as a tough sailer. It was very difficult to bring her about. Her homeport was in Boston, Massachusetts. She had a successful career as a coal carrier but when she was converted to carry oil she was lost on her first trip across the Atlantic. She arrived off the coast of England in a storm. She anchored and then dragged ashore and was wrecked with the loss of seventeen men. Only two persons survived the wreck. *Photo courtesy of the Smithsonian Institution, Washington, D.C.* **Below:** The drawing depicts the Life Savers launching in high seas to rescue the crew of a grounded four-masted schooner off the New England coast. *Drawing by Paul C. Morris, Nantucket, Massachusetts.*

Above: The remains of the concrete steamer *Polias*, 2,565 tons, 267 feet long. She was wrecked in Penobscot Bay on Old Cilley ledge off Port Clyde in a blizzard on the night of February 6, 1920. Eleven of her crew were lost when they set out in a lifeboat during the storm. The next morning the Coast Guard cutter *Acushnet* saved the remaining 27 crewmen and brought them to Rockland. The hull sat on the ledge and deteriorated to a grotesque form in the middle of the bay. *Photo courtesy of Bath Marine Museum, Bath, Maine.* **Below:** The wreckers at work. This is a deck view of the wrecking lighter *Addie,* getting ready to refloat the three-masted schooner *William Booth* off the rocks at Nobska Point near Woods Hole on Cape Cod in March, 1921. The workmen are getting the 9,500 lb. anchor ready for setting. The big rope in the foreground is an 18'' hawser used for the beach gear. Beach gear is a rig consisting of anchors, buoys, hawser and tackle used to haul stranded vessels afloat. Wrecking barges are equipped with booms, a hoisting engine, pumps and a shallow draft to get in close to work on the wrecks. *Photo courtesy of Bob Beattie.*

Above: On the evening trip from New York to Bridgeport, Connecticut, on February 4, 1920, the steamer *Maine* plowed into the thick pack ice in Long Island Sound. The ice was over four feet thick and stopped up the condenser water intake on the ship. The vessel lost power and was stopped in the ice. A northeast snowstorm was raging and the turn of the tide carried the *Maine* onto a ledge near Execution Rocks punching a hole in her bottom and filling the lower deck. The steamer settled to the bottom with the water above the freight deck.

The passengers and crew were stranded on board for three days without much heat and then a freight lighter worked her way to the steamer through the ice and removed the passengers and a dozen or so horses. Officials of the New England Steamship Company surveyed the steamer and found that salvage was going to be too expensive so they ordered her stripped and abandoned. **Below:** Because of the danger of fire and the proximity to the lighthouse the upper wooden superstructure was burned to get rid of it. With the wind just right, wreckers touched off the wood and within eight minutes the whole vessel was involved. The fuel was eastern white pine, 29 years old with many coats of white paint and in a few short hours all of the wood was burned away leaving metal parts for salvage. A sorry end for a once proud steamer. *Photos courtesy of Bob Beattie.*

Above: The British tramp steamer *Wandby,* bound from Algiers to Portland, Maine, in ballast, ran aground in dense fog at Kennebunkport on March 9, 1921. The vessel lay on the rocks for months. The hull was finally cut up for scrap. *Photo courtesy of the Bath Marine Museum, Bath, Maine.* **Below:** Built in Portsmouth, New Hampshire between 1819 and 1825, the *New Hampshire,* later the *Granite State,* a 74 gun ship of the line was being used by the New York state naval militia as a barracks ship when she caught fire on May 23, 1921, and sank at the pier on the Hudson River. She was raised and sold for scrap. The ship was being towed to the Bay of Fundy when she sank in a storm off Graves Island near Cape Ann, Massachusetts. New England "*Scuba*" divers have brought up from this vessel many copper spikes said to have been wrought in Paul Revere's foundry. *Photo from the collection of Paul C. Morris, Nantucket, Massachusetts.*

94

Above: At 1:30 a.m., Sunday, Sept. 18, 1921, about six miles south of Montauk Shoals, off Long Island, N.Y., in thick fog the steam collier *Malden* was in collision with the *S.S. Johancy*. The *Malden* suffered a large hole in her port side forward of the bridge. An SOS was radioed, and salvage tugs arrived on scene the next morning and took the *Malden* in tow. That evening the ship sank onto a sand bar just east of Washington Shoal, near Montauk Point at the tip of Long Island. A few days on the bar and it was decided to abandon the vessel. Later the Coast Guard destroyed her as she was a menace to navigation. *Photo by Bob Beattie.* **Below:** The five-masted schooner *Sintram,* bound from Philadelphia for Portland with 3,764 tons of coal came into Muskegat channel between Martha's Vineyard and Nantucket Islands early in the morning of November 15, 1921, bound over the shoals for Pollock Rip when the wind died out and she drifted with the flood tide and ran aground on Hawes shoal. Bob Beattie aboard the tug *Guardsman* made this photograph on the next day when the tug pulled her out of the sand. She was towed into Vineyard Haven harbor and inspected by divers and on the 18th set sail and headed north again. Early in the morning of the 19th the steamer *David McKelvy* rammed the schooner in heavy fog off Cape Cod, and the *Sintram* went to the bottom. Her crew of 12 men was saved by the steamer.

The four-masted schooner *Gladys M. Taylor* was grounded on the shoals, north-northeast of Cross Rip lightship in Nantucket Sound on November 5, 1921, Bob Beattie, a crewman aboard the tug *Guardsman* made this photograph as she was pulled free of the sand bar.

The four-masted Canadian schooner *Bessie A. White* bound from Newport News, Virginia to St. John, New Brunswick, went aground on February 6, 1922 one mile west of Smith's Point, Long Island, N.Y. Life savers landed the crew, and wreckers were notified. The vessel was full of water, and, subsequently, ship and cargo were a total loss. *Photo courtesy of the Mariners Museum, Newport News, Virginia.*

About 3 a.m. on May 19, 1922, the United States Navy Eagle Boat #17 ran aground near Ammagansett, Long Island, New York. The Navy craft was in pursuit of a rumrunner near shore in haze. The rummy lured the ship too close in and she sheared off her propeller trying to back out off the bar. The 64-man crew was rescued by the United States Coast Guard from the Georgica Station by the breeches buoy. The ship was a total loss and the rumrunner got away. *Photo by Bob Beattie.*

The roaring '20s began on January 16, 1920, when the 18th amendment to the United States Constitution became the law of the land. Prohibition arrived and the country went dry according to the law. This was to have a profound effect on the coastal waters of New England. Captain Bill McCoy created ''Rum Row'' just outside the three mile limit in the Atlantic ocean. A line of rumrunners loaded with illegal whiskey supplied small boats from the mainland. McCoy bought and sold only high quality liquors; hence the expression ''the real McCoy.'' His 40 m.p.h. speedboats left the Coast Guard way behind in their wakes. Millionaires were made overnight as contraband liquor, smuggled in darkness, became big business. The Coast Guard soon acquired better equipment to handle the problem and began a war on the whiskey dealers of the deep.

The smugglers got faster boats, and the Coast Guard were issued some old World War I four stack destroyers and were nicknamed the ''Prohibition Navy.'' Sometimes the illicit cargoes had to be thrown overboard to lighten the boat in order to escape arrest. Beachcombing became a highly lucrative occupation at times when the jettisoned cases of liquor floated ashore. There were numerous wrecks on both the Atlantic and Pacific coasts, the St. Lawrence River, and the Great Lakes. Both the smugglers and the Coast Guard lost vessels in the rum war. There were, at times, battles on the high seas with guns blazing killing several on both sides of the whiskey conflict.

On February 3, 1924, two speedy launches loaded with $50,000 worth of liquor were headed for shore near Hull, Massachusetts. They were about to rendezvous with their confederates on shore when Coast Guardsmen from the Point Allerton station arrived at the scene. The smugglers in the launches spotted the Coast Guardsmen and immediately turned back and headed out to sea in a snowstorm. They disappeared from sight tossing cases of whiskey into the sea. Later the wreckage of the two boats was found on the rocks near Boston Light. The crewmen were not found and their fate was unknown.

The Nova Scotia four-masted schooner *Ada Tower* came ashore at Sayville, Long Island, New York on May 23, 1923. The Bay of Fundy vessels were built to take good ground with no damage. The sandy shores of Long Island did no damage to the hull and the *Tower* was pulled off the beach and went back to sea. *Photo courtesy of Paul C. Morris, Nantucket, Massachusetts.*

The rumrunners that were apprehended and brought into court usually would go free on the finding of a sympathetic jury of their peers, who did not want to cut off their own supply of liquor. Following the trials, they were back on the high seas again the next night, bringing in more whiskey and gin. Customs and Prohibition agents were diligent in their fight against the illegal flow of liquor into the country, but ever increasing numbers of people were engaging in smuggling and the tide never seemed to ebb for the persistent Federal men. Society, in general, deteriorated during this time. Herbert Hoover described it as "The Noble Experiment." Prohibition ushered in the era of the gangster.

Above: The steamer *City of Rockland* had a career marked by frequent disasters. They include groundings and collisions with other Maine steamers. The accident that finished the vessel was the time she piled up on ledges off Cox's Point at the mouth of the Kennebec River on September 2, 1923. After she lay on the ledges for several days the Merritt Chapman Company refloated her and brought her to Boston where the survey decided that repairs would be too expensive and she was abandoned. *Photo courtesy of Paul C. Morris, Nantucket, Massachusetts.* **Below:** On September 9, 1923, at 3:30 a.m. the steam collier *Everett* rammed into the schooner *Frederick J. Lovatt* on the port side abreast the main rigging and cut into the main hatch and down to the keel. The ships were in Vineyard Sound, three miles east of Hedge Fence lightship. The crew remained on board atop the after cabin as the ship was towed, decks awash, into Vineyard Haven harbor by Coast Guard cutters. The vessel was raised and towed to Boston two weeks later. *Photo courtesy of the Mariners Museum, Newport News, Virginia.*

Another giant coal schooner was wrecked on January 12, 1924, when the picturesque *Ruth E. Merrill* grounded on L'Hommedieu Shoal in Vineyard Sound. The vessel had a cargo of 5,000 tons of coal. The 20-year old ship had been battling a storm and her seams worked open. The pumps could not keep up with the flooding and she sank on the shoal. The crew of thirteen came ashore at Woods Hole in the ship's boat. The *Merrill*, a total loss, was one of the largest schooners in the world. *Photo courtesy of the Maine Maritime Museum, Bath, Maine.*

Above: On January 26, 1924, the steamer *Gov. Bodwell* ran up on Spindle Ledge near Swan's Island in a blinding snow storm. Distress signals brought out the island fishermen who removed the passengers and mail. The vessel was later salvaged and rebuilt to steam Maine waters for a few more years. *Photo from the collection of Frank E. Claes, Orland, Maine.* **Below:** The largest six-masted (G.T.) schooner was the *Wyoming*. Launched in 1909 she was 3,730 gross tons, 329.5 ft. in length, 50.1 ft. in beam and 30.4 ft. in depth. She carried 6,000 tons of coal. On March 11, 1924, the vessel was caught in a blizzard in Nantucket Sound and lost with all on board. The loss occurred at night while the ship was at anchor near Pollock Rip Lightship. Thirteen men were lost in the tragedy. Parts of the wreckage washed ashore on Nantucket Island. *Photo courtesy of the Mariners Museum, Newport News, Virginia.*

The *SS Grand Republic*, sister ship to the *General Slocum,* sunk on the left in the above photo, was one of the five vessels destroyed by fire early in the morning of April 26, 1924, at their winter berth in the Hudson River off 157th Street, New York City. The fire started in the *SS C.A.M. Church* and spread to the *SS Highlander* and the lighter Nassau and the towboat *Barton.* Several thousand persons were attracted to the scene by the flames leaping into the air. Fire companies from all over the city responded to additional alarms, but the boats could not be saved. *Photo courtesy of the Steamship Historical Society of America, Viez collection.*

In the years 1921-22 commercial radio stations went on the air all over the country. Music, news and sports events were brought into America's living rooms as the age of radio arrived. In other news, the shipping industry found that Prohibition caused more problems. Coupled with the post war decline, American ships could not get cargoes at foreign ports, and passenger service was affected because United States ships could not serve liquor on board. At this time the transatlantic liners were converting from coal to oil, thus cutting the crews needed in the boiler rooms by ninety percent. In May of 1921, a labor dispute tied up ship traffic along the east coast of the United States for two months.

In April, 1922, three enterprising men from Gloucester bought the *John Finnanhaddie,* a used fishing trawler that was in need of rebuilding. Before they overhauled the vessel they decided to make a quick fishing trip to Georges Bank to earn enough money to pay for the repairs needed to put the boat in first class condition. On the way out, she developed engine trouble and caught fire. The crew could not control the fire, and the captain suffered a compound fracture of his leg when it was fouled in a chain. The crew hastily abandoned the vessel and just did make it into a dory, but with no oars, food or water. They had drifted for three days and nights, riding out a gale, when they were spotted by Robert Beattie, a crewman aboard the tug *Guardsman.* The tug saved the men and brought them ashore at Newport, Rhode Island, where they were rushed to a hospital, much the sadder but a little wiser.

On March 30, 1924, the Fire Island lightship was again rammed. The British freighter *Castillian* crashed into the side of the lightship in dense fog, ripping a jagged hole on the port side just above the water line. Distress signals were sent, but both vessels could proceed. The lighthouse tender *Spruce* was sent to convoy the lightship into New York harbor for repairs because of the threat of strong head winds.

Above: The new Eastern Steamship liner *Boston* was nearly lost when she was struck on her port side by the tanker *Swift Arrow* in dense fog off Point Judith, Rhode Island, on July 21, 1924. Four passengers were killed in the collision. The *Boston* was bound for New York City with 700 persons on board. The Fall River Line steamers *Priscilla, Providence,* and *Plymouth* picked up the passengers while the giant steamer *Commonwealth* came alongside and tied up to the *Boston* and, with the help of two navy tugs from the Newport naval base, brought the sinking liner into Newport harbor and grounded her on the mud flats. *Photo courtesy of the Steamship Historical Society of America.* **Below:** With the two navy tugs alongside the *Boston* with her lifeboats in tow rests on the mud flats. The ship was repaired and went back into service. *Photo courtesy of the Mariners Museum, Newport News, Virginia.*

104

The largest steamer to sail on the Long Island Sound. The *Commonwealth* displaced 5,410 tons. She was one of the most popular overnight vessels on the run between New York and New England. *Photo courtesy of the Steamship Historical Society of America, Viez collection.*

Navigators following the New England charts have no trouble finding their way and even though they are unfamiliar with the local areas, they know the dangerous places just by the unique names the New Englanders have given to spots like "Cutthroat Shoal" and "Wreck Ledge." In Maine there is "Deadman Point" and "Drunkard Ledge." The derivation of some of the names is lost in the folklore, but one of the legends passed down is about a man named Bailey. The story goes that Captain Bailey ran aground one night and in the morning he found his schooner high and dry. They couldn't get the schooner off and since then that area has been known as "Bailey's Mistake." It's so listed on all Maine charts to this day. Still there are others like "Toothacher Cove," "Devil's Elbow," "Quicksand Point" and "Hell Gate."

It is not difficult to imagine how some of the names came to be. At the end of Long Island Sound is an area known as "Execution Rocks." Stories passed down over the years relate that, during the Revolutionary War, the English Governor wanted to eliminate some influential but troublesome Patriots quietly without incurring the wrath of the populace. The Patriots were lured out in a boat to go fishing, and then taken to the rock where at low tide, they were chained to the big boulders. When the tide came in they were drowned. Their cries for help were too far from shore to be heard. Many Patriots were executed this way according to the stories told about "Execution Rocks."

Statistics released in July of 1925 showed fewer shipwrecks reported in the previous year. The use of the wireless radio and the increased efficiency of life saving equipment in general were listed as the reasons for the decline. In October of 1925, a block of wood washed ashore on Martha's Vineyard Island off the coast of Massachusetts. Scratched into the wood were details of the loss of the schooner *Norka,* which occurred in the mid Atlantic in August. The writing said that this was the last hope of five survivors adrift in an open boat on August 2nd about 1,000 miles east-southeast of Boston. The message was signed by five sets of initials. The *Norka* was listed in the registers as a schooner yacht of 28 tons, hailing from New York.

The Gloucester fishing schooner *Evelyn & Ralph* came ashore in dense fog on the south shore of Nantucket on December 6, 1924. An odd accident happened on board when the vessel struck the bar. The foc's'l'e stove tipped over and set the boat afire. She was a total loss. *Photo courtesy of Charlie Sayle, Nantucket, Massachusetts.* **Below:** A rumrunner lost his bearings and then lost his vessel in Muskegat channel. On December 26, 1924, the Canadian schooner *Waldo L. Stream* with 2,295 cases of whiskey on board grounded on the shoals near Muskegat, off Nantucket, Massachusetts. The crew tossed over half of the cargo over the side to lighten the vessel and refloat her. The attempt was unsuccessful and the crew was taken from the vessel by the Coast Guard from the Muskegat Station. The hull was smashed by the surf pounding her. The whiskey was "spirited" away somehow. *Photo courtesy of the Mariners Museum, Newport News, Virginia.*

Above: The schooner *W.N. Reinhardt* fighting a gale off Cape Cod lost her sails and rudder and struck the beach at Race Point at Provincetown at 1:30 a.m. on December 7, 1926. The crew were frostbitten and were taken to the Coast Guard station for medical aid. The cargo of lumber and lath was strewn over the beach. *Photo courtesy of Allie Ryan.* **Below:** The storm raged on and in three days the main and mizzen masts were down but wreckers salvaged most of the cargo. The hull was a total loss. *Photo by United States Coast Guard in the National Archives.*

A severe northeast gale with seventy m.p.h. winds caused havoc along the Massachusetts coastline on February 21, 1927. The five-masted schooner *Nancy* had anchored outside Boston Lightship and was driven ashore at Nantasket with her anchors dragging. A group of volunteers manned the Massachusetts Humane Society's boat and successfully removed the crew of nine. *Photos courtesy of the Mariners Museum, Newport News, Virginia.*

Above: The *Nancy* continued to earn money as she lay on the beach. Crowds flocked to the ship on Sundays. Adults paid 25 cents and children 15 cents to go aboard. A photographer set up a camera to make photographs of people with the ship in the background. *Photo courtesy of the Mariners Museum, Newport News, Virginia.* **Below:** The *Nancy's* hull stayed on the beach throughout the 1930's and became an advertising medium. The hull was finally burned. *Photo by R. Loren Graham, courtesy of the Steamship Historical Society of America.*

Above: In a blinding snowstorm on February 14, 1927, the Gloucester fishing schooner *Elsie G. Silva* foundered on the outer Cape Cod beach near Pamet River in Truro. The crew of 20 men abandoned the vessel in five dories. They all made it ashore safely with the aid of the Coast Guard. *Photo by True Fife.* **Below:** The schooner *Camilla May Page* grounded on the rocks at Jefferey's Point at the entrance to Portsmouth, New Hampshire Harbor on November 18, 1928. The vessel had a full load of coal on board and was leaking badly. A couple of weeks later, storm seas destroyed the schooner after only 15 tons of coal had been recovered. *From the collection of Paul C. Morris, Nantucket, Massachusetts.*

Above: On the snowy night of March 9, 1928, the Eastern Steamship liner *Robert E. Lee* grounded on the Mary Ann rocks off Manomet Point near Plymouth, Mass. None of the 263 passengers was injured, but a Coast Guard surfboat from the Manomet station capsized while returning to the station from the wreck, and three of her seven man crew were lost in the high seas. The liner remained on the rocks for seven weeks before salvage crews from the Merritt Chapman & Scott Co., managed to pull her free and tow the ship to Boston. *Photo courtesy of the Mariners Museum, Newport News, Virginia.* **Below:** On January 26, 1929, the British steamer *Silvermaple* battling gale winds and high seas suffered a broken rudder and lost her steering 780 miles east of Boston, Massachusetts. The Coast Guard cutters *Mojave* and *Tampa* went to her aid and towed the crippled steamer to Bermuda. The wrecking tug *Willet* took over the tow and brought her to New York arriving on February 23rd. The *Silvermaple* carried a five million dollar cargo of rubber products. *Photo courtesy of United States Coast Guard in the National Archives.*

On November 29, 1929, five of six steamers of the Nantasket Beach line were destroyed by fire. The vessels were tied to the dock at Nantasket Pier in Hull, Massachusetts. The only vessel saved from the conflagration was the steamer *Mayflower*. The pier and surrounding property suffered a million dollars in damage. *Photos courtesy of the Mariners Museum, Newport News, Virginia.*

Above: The steamer *Mayflower,* in her better days, passing East Boston with a full load of passengers. *Author's collection.* **Below:** When the passenger business declined the *Mayflower* was tied to the dock for a few years. In the late 1940's she was put on dry land and became the Showboat Mayflower. The years took their toll and in 1979 the hull was scheduled for demolition. *Photo by William P. Quinn.*

Phenomenal luck and good seamanship averted a major disaster in August, 1926. In thick fog at midnight, the eastbound Cunard liner *Samaria* narrowly avoided a collision with the westbound Anchor liner *Cameronia* thirty-seven miles west of the Nantucket lightship. Captain Robert Smart of the *Cameronia* was credited with "coolness and presence of mind" to avert a disaster, with 1,500 persons involved on both ships. It was estimated that the two ships passed with only six feet of space between them. Passengers on both ships expressed fear and apprehension after the incident. Capt. Smart stated that he had heard the whistle of the other ship and had immediately altered course to avoid collision with the eastbound liner. All on board talked about the close call and lauded Capt. Smart's skill and quick action in saving his ship.

In May of 1927, Charles A. Lindbergh made history. He was the first man to fly solo across the Atlantic Ocean. He flew from Roosevelt Field, Long Island and landed at LeBourget Air Field in Paris, 33½ hours later and became an instant hero throughout the world. On August 5, 1929, the German *Graf Zeppelin* landed at Lakehurst, New Jersey after a 93 hour flight from Germany. Passengers remarked that "it sure beats steamships." They told about the comfortable ride, the good food, and that they slept well. The dirigible was just beginning in the Atlantic passenger trade and might have flourished had not the United States collapsed financially.

On October 29, 1929, the New York stock market crashed plunging the country into its worst depression in history. Banks failed all over the land, and soon hard times spread to other countries throughout the world. Unemployment was at its highest peak, but the motor cars continued to roll all over the United States. Comedian Will Rogers said: "We are the only country in history to go to the poor house in an automobile." The dismal conditions in America brought on the bread lines and the poverty of the 1930's.

CHAPTER SEVEN

The freighter *Edward Luckenbach* ran aground on Block Island in dense fog on January 10, 1930. The rocks tore open the hull, and, historically, vessels in this position have been pounded to pieces in a matter of hours. This vessel, however, was lucky and weathered the heavy winter seas and was refloated three months later on March 5, 1930. *Photo from the collection of Paul C. Morris, Nantucket, Massachusetts.*

A deep economic crisis opened the 1930's in the country. The United States had made big strides in her climb to become an industrial giant. The wealth of this country was vast. We enjoyed the highest standard of living of the time, backed by a plentiful and healthy labor force, sound business leadership, inventive skills, mass production, an excellent educational system and the best transportation and communications in the world. However, these alone could not insure against flaws in the system. When the balance of the economy was upset as in 1929 when producers overproduced and consumers underconsumed, chaos ensued. Many years passed before the economy returned to normal. When the stock market finally hit bottom in 1932 the loss was recorded at about 75 billion dollars.

In other news of the decade the George Washington Bridge opened in 1931 over the Hudson River in New York City and the nation's railroads were spending money to improve service to meet the challenge of the airlines for passengers. Steamship travel was still in a decline. The depression got worse. In 1932 Franklin D. Roosevelt was elected president. The new president brought forth a "New Deal" for the country with "pump-priming" legislation, and then took the country off the gold standard. At this time, advocates declared that dirigible travel across the ocean was fast and safe, but they rode on a sea of hydrogen gas - a highly explosive element.

On December 5, 1933, the United States Coast Guard ended a fourteen year battle with the rumrunners. Prohibition was over. Liquor flowed freely again, after a war vigorously waged and well fought by the Coast Guard. However, it was similar to an army patrol taking on a battalion. They were far outnumbered, but they upheld the traditions of the service and did their best with what they had to work with and remained steadfast to the end. In December of 1934, in an economy move, shipping companies stopped the practice of delivering Christmas plum puddings to arriving overseas vessels and to clerks and pier police. One clerk agonized in his report that it was a "plum pity."

Above: In Provincetown, Massachusetts, the Peaked Hill Bars Life Saving Station became a victim of erosion. The building had been abandoned by the Government Service for a newer facility shown in the distant background. *Photo courtesy of the Cape Cod National Seashore.*
Below: Late on the night of March 18, 1931, the British freighter *Silveryew* rammed head on into the small coastal freighter *Arminda* in lower New York harbor. Officials could not determine the cause of the accident as it was a clear night and visibility was good. Seven men asleep in the fo'c's'le were injured, one seriously with a broken back, when the collision occurred. The extent of the damage is clearly visible with the ship in drydock. *Photo courtesy of the Steamship Historical Society of America, Viez collection.*

Above: The island steamer *Naushon* altered course to avoid a collision in Vineyard Haven harbor on August 24, 1931, and was caught by 50 m.p.h. winds and forced ashore. A variety of other craft were caught in the accident, including the coastal schooner *Alice S. Wentworth* whose bowsprit went into the after gangway and in the freight deck. A couple of tugs pulled her off the next day with little damage. *Photo courtesy of Jack Hough, The Falmouth Enterprise.* **Below:** The steamer *Albertina* (walking beam in the smoky background) caught fire on the morning of May 9, 1932, and the fire extended to the steamer *Sea Bird* and to the surrounding lumber piers at 152nd Street on the East River, New York City. Fire fighters may be seen pouring water on the smoldering vessels. The *Sea Bird* was built in 1886. Both steamers were a total loss. *Photo courtesy of the Peabody Museum of Salem, Massachusetts.*

Above: On August 6, 1932, two island steamers collided in Nantucket Sound in dense fog. The drawing depicts the moment of collision as the *Nantucket* rammed into the *Martha's Vineyard*. Damage was not extensive on either ship as they were under reduced speed in the thick weather. *Drawing by Bill Ewen, Jr., Providence, Rhode Island.* **Below:** The *Nantucket* had to go to Simpsons yard in East Boston to have a new bow installed. Service to the islands was interrupted during repairs to both vessels. *Photo by R. Loren Graham, courtesy of the Steamship Historical Society of America.*

On December 20, 1933, the three-masted schooner *Granville R. Bacon* came ashore on Weekapaug Point, Rhode Island, in thick weather. In the driving rain the Captain mistook a street lamp for a light on a passing steamer. The crew of six was saved by the Coast Guard. The ship was a total loss. *Photo by Robert H.I. Goddard, Providence, Rhode Island.*

Above: The Eastern Steamship Lines' freighter *Sagamore*, 2,599 tons, with a crew of 26 headed out of Portland, Maine, at midnight on January 14, 1934, bound for New York in a northeast blizzard, with promises of improving weather. The freighter later ran up on Corwin's Rock, four miles off shore as her look-outs could not spot Willard Rock light buoy, which was out at the time. The hull was leaking badly, and it was decided to beach the vessel. She came ashore on a reef off Prouts Neck, Maine. The Coast Guard sent a boat out the next morning to remove her crew. The cargo was salvaged but the ship was a total loss. *Photo from the Ballard Collection by Ralph Blood.* **Below:** The coastal freighter *Northern Sword* anchored in President Roads outside Boston Harbor during a driving blizzard on February 21, 1934, snapped the anchor chains and drifted onto a rocky ledge off Winthrop. There was some minor hull damage but no injuries to her crew of 35 men. She was pulled off a few days later by the salvage tug *Resolute* of the Merritt Chapman & Scott Co. of New York and towed to the Simpson Drydock in East Boston for inspection. *Photo by R. Loren Graham, courtesy of Steamship Historical Society of America.*

Drawing by Paul C. Morris, Nantucket, Massachusetts

The Nantucket lightship is moored at one of the most isolated and exposed stations in the world. On May 15, 1934, the White Star liner *Olympic* was proceeding in dense fog toward New York City and following the lightship's radio beacon, a combination radio-compass signal, used by ships with radio direction finders to proceed on their course in limited visibility. The instrument aboard the liner was extremely accurate that morning when at about eleven a.m. the *Olympic* loomed out of the fog and cut the lightship in half. The crewmen aboard the lightship had only a 30 second warning of the disaster and hardly had time to don life jackets. Seven men died, and the lightship sank in less than a minute at her station 43 miles southeast of Nantucket Island. The *Olympic* stopped and picked up four survivors and three bodies. The bodies of the other four men went down with the ship and were not recovered. Survivor Captain George Braithwaite of the lightship told of the crew having been up all night, as there were two close calls with other steamers on the previous evening. Normally, ships using the RDF would pass no closer than a quarter of a mile away from the lightship. It was ironic that the radio beacons and direction finders that were designed to save lives would be the major cause of the disaster.

Above: The stern of the United Fruit steamship *Atenas* settled to the bottom beside the North River pier in New York City following a six hour battle by land and marine fire forces to put out the fire in the after holds. The blaze of undetermined origin occurred on July 27, 1934, and caused a half million dollar loss. The ship was later raised. *Photo courtesy of the Mariners Museum, Newport News, Virginia.* **Below:** On September 30, 1934, the island steamer *New Bedford* struck Weepecket Rock near Woods Hole, Massachusetts. The ship was leaking badly; so her captain ran her ashore on nearby Uncatena Island. Her passengers were removed by the local small craft, and a few days later with pumps working aboard the *New Bedford* the tug *Resolute* pulled her free and towed her to drydocks for repairs. *Photo from the collection of Paul Ç. Morris, Nantucket.*

Below: The 43 year old *King Philip,* a famous Boston excursion boat succumbed to old age and sank at her berth at T wharf in January of 1935.
Right: In April, a Merritt Chapman derrick raised her and carried her out of the harbor to be sunk at a proper gravesite, deep in Massachusetts Bay, east of the Graves light. *Photos courtesy of the Steamship Historical Society of America.*

Above: One signal for distress is to fly the national ensign upside down. The tug *Diamond,* in the trough of the seas with only her top hamper showing was assisted by the Coast Guard into New York harbor on December 10, 1935. *Photo by the United States Coast Guard in the National Archives, Washington, D.C.* **Below:** The 5,399 ton freighter *Canadian Planter* was in collision with the freighter *City of Auckland* late at night on May 3, 1936, in dense fog and sank on Horseshoe Shoal in Nantucket Sound. There were some tense moments after the accident until all of the engine room crew escaped the lower decks. The captain of the *City of Auckland* held his vessel to the side of the *Canadian Planter* until the crew of the sinking vessel transferred to his ship. The damaged freighter then drifted over to the south side of the shoal and sank to her decks. Most of the cargo was lost, but the vessel was later salvaged. *Photo courtesy of Paul C. Morris, Nantucket, Massachusetts.*

The palatial steamer *Iroquois* ran up on Bald Porcupine Island at Bar Harbor, Maine, in dense fog at 3:30 a.m. on July 12, 1936. The ship was underway for New York City at the time. Her steel bow was almost up in the trees. After daylight the 180 passengers were taken off and had to make the New York trip by train. That afternoon after a hole in the bow was sealed with plank and timber, the ship was pulled off on the high tide by the United States minesweeper *Owl*. Repairs were made later in New York City. *Photo courtesy of the Steamship Historical Society of America.*

On January 6, 1935, strange smoke signals were seen just above the fog blanket on Great South Bay near Patchogue, Long Island, New York. There was a 30' sloop icebound in the bay, and a local resident reported seeing smoke signals, Indian style, reading S O S coming from the cookstove chimney. The Coast Guard sent an icebreaker to the area, but they could not find the sloop in the dense fog and thick ice. On August 13, 1935, a hit and run incident in the North Atlantic occurred as the Boston trawler *Patrick J. O'Hara* was fishing in fog on the western banks off Nova Scotia. A large steamship rammed the trawler on the starboard side. The impact heeled the smaller vessel over until the port rail was under water. The fishing vessel righted herself and her Captain, Patrick McCue of Boston, blew his whistle to attract attention, but the unknown steamer continued in the fog and did not stop.

A hurricane swept across Newfoundland in August, 1935, and the toll rose to over fifty fishermen lost. Ships were pounded against the rocky coast. Crews were washed overboard by huge waves. Derelict fishing boats were found all over the North Atlantic, and, tragically, five brothers were lost on one vessel off the Avalon Peninsula.

The lightship service found that accidents came in threes in 1935. In early April the Nantucket lightship was torn from her station in a storm and lost her anchors and chains. The ship went into New Bedford for repairs. On September 17, the Grace liner *Santa Barbara* collided in haze with the Ambrose lightship outside New York harbor. The accident crumpled the bow of the lightship back 14 feet into her main deck. Both ships limped into the harbor for repairs. On December 20th the British freighter *Seven Seas* rammed the Boston lightship and badly damaged the vessel seven miles outside Boston harbor in clear weather at about nine in the morning. The lightship was leaking badly and it was towed to a Quincy drydock for repairs. The reason for the accident was rumored to be sabotage. The Captain of the freighter told officials that the steering gear suddenly failed. The Government filed at $20,000 damage claim against the British vessel.

The Norwegian steamship *Kings County* ran on the rocks near Lornville, New Brunswick, in darkness, fog, and rain on December 10, 1936. The wind and a strong tide drew the vessel off her course. One member of the crew became a hero when he swam through the mountainous seas 100 feet to the cliff and shore with a rope which he tied to a large boulder. The crew then made the rope fast on the mast and went ashore hand over hand on the life line. The ship was a total loss. *Photo by John Lochhead, courtesy of the Mariners Museum, Newport News, Virginia.*

Late at night on December 12, 1936, the ship *King's County* drifted off her course and struck the rocks off Lorneville, New Brunswick. The seas were running very high and it was impossible to launch lifeboats. The hull was being ground to pieces on the rocks, and the crew were in peril of their lives. A 26 year old Norwegian seaman, Harold Hansen stripped off all but his pants, tied a rope around his waist and dove into the sea and swam for shore about 100 feet away. The waves dashed him about and he was caught in undertow in the icy waters. It took him over fifteen minutes to reach shore, and he was almost smashed to death on the rocky cliffs but he grabbed an outcrop of smooth rocks and gained dry land. He tied the rope to a large boulder, and the rest of the crew went to safety over the line, one by one, hand over hand until all 35 men were safely ashore. Cold, tired and wet, they spent the night on the rocks as no lights were visible anywhere. The next morning they walked to the nearby village and were given shelter and warm food. Seaman Hansen was a hero to his shipmates who would have all perished had it not been for his super strength and fortitude. The ship was a total loss.

In 1937, business, in general, was on the upturn. The depression was almost over, and people were traveling again. Zepplins were flying across the ocean in ever increasing regularity, and their business was good. However, on May 6, a spectacular accident occurred at Lakehurst, New Jersey, when the *Hindenburg* burst into flames while trying to land. Thirty-six persons died in the holocaust. This ended commercial dirigible flights. Officials of the German airship company charged sabotage, but it was never proved as any evidence went up in flames in the disaster.

During the 1930's the United States labor movement prospered. Industrial unions organized and the Committee for Industrial Organization (C.I.O.) was formed. Not all of the workers won their arguments against management however. In the summer of 1937, the Fall River Line workers went out on a sitdown strike. With huge operating losses and stiffer competition, the owners decided to toss in the towel. They closed up shop, dissolved the company, and sold the boats. The workers were left sitting on the docks, wondering what happened. Automobiles, the railroads and the airlines were providing quicker and safer transportation than the steamers; so the coastal passenger steamboats began to go the way of the sailing vessel.

Above: The steamer *Cherokee* built in 1892, opened up her seams and sank at the dock on East 7th Street in New York City on November 8, 1936. *Photo courtesy of the Peabody Museum of Salem.* **Below:** After the Federal Government took over the operations of the Cape Cod Canal, Congress decided to widen and deepen the canal. On January 27, 1937, the dredge *Governor Herrick* sprang a leak and sank while extracting a huge boulder from the bottom of the canal. The dredge was out of the ship channel and did not stop traffic. It was subsequently raised. *Photo courtesy of the United States Army Engineers, Cape Cod Canal.*

U.S. ENGINEERS
Cape Cod Canal, Buzzards Bay, Mass.
Contract No. W175 Eng.-596
Arundal Corp. 9-yd. dredge "Governor Herrick" sunk in canal. Built 1912.
Length 130' beam 48' bow 45' stern.

Going in the River 49
At. Cape Girardeau Mo.
1937 Coast Guard Flood Duty.

58 Coast Guard Standing By
1937 Flood Stage 59.8'
Cairo. Ill.

On January 25, 1937, about 40 motor launches from the first Coast Guard district were loaded onto flat cars at the Boston Navy yard for transportation to the flooded areas in the mid-west. The Coast Guard crews boarded the train on January 26th and later arrived in Illinois where some of the boats were off-loaded by crane while others were floated by running the flat cars into the rising waters. The boats then traveled in a convoy down river to Paducah, Kentucky and then to Cairo, Illinois. Upon arrival at Cairo, the contingent was split up. Some boats were sent to Kentucky and others to Missouri, while still others went to Memphis, Tennessee.

Underway for a week with the flood waters still rising, the boats were assigned to assist flood victims. At the height of the flood there was sixty feet of water over sections of Paducah, Kentucky. In Missouri the boats at one point worked for three days and nights endlessly evacuating stranded persons and rendering assistance. In the twelve states affected, 12,700 square miles were under flood waters. Two hundred-fifty persons lost their lives and there was three hundred million dollars in property damage. On February 11th, the flood waters crested and slowly began to recede. The Coast Guard contingent were ordered back to New England and the boats and men returned by train and arrived in Boston to resume their regular duties on February 18th. *Photographs and data courtesy of Lieut. Benjamin F. Lombard, U.S.C.G. [Ret.] Natick, Massachusetts.*

1. Mounds City Ill. 1937
Flood Stage 59.8'

"River Stay 'Way From My Door" 17.
Mounds City. Ill. Flood Stage 60'

Above: On March 23, 1937, a workman's acetylene torch touched off a $30,000 fire at the Simpson's Plant of Bethlehem Shipyard in East Boston, Massachusetts. Tugs and fireboats rushed to the scene of the five-alarm blaze which threatened three ships at the yard. This photograph was taken from the Custom House tower in Boston. Damage from the fire was to the wooden pier, a crane, a floating drydock and the United Fruit steamer *San Gil*. *Photo from the R. Loren Graham collection, courtesy of the Steamship Historical Society of America.* **Below:** The freighter *Capillo* went aground on Shovelful Shoal off Monomoy Point south of Cape Cod, Massachusetts, on July 28, 1937. The Coast Guard cutters *Faunce* and *Algonquin* rigged hawsers and pulled the ship off the shoals. *Photo courtesy of Paul C. Morris, Nantucket, Massachusetts.*

Above: The tug *Plymouth* sunk at the east end of the Cape Cod Canal following a collision with the collier *Everett* on January 27, 1938. The accident occurred in the evening and sixteen men were thrown into the icy waters of the canal. Nearby small craft rushed to the aid of the men and fifteen men were saved and one man was lost. The barge that was being towed was tied to piers shown in the background of the photograph. The tug was raised later. *Photo courtesy of the Corps of Engineers at the Cape Cod Canal.* **Below:** The famous zoo ship, the *City of Salisbury*, broke in half on Graves ledge outside Boston Harbor. The ship ran up on the shoals in dense fog on April 22, 1938, while trying to enter the harbor with a cargo of exotic animals and other cargo. The animals were removed, and the vessel became a tourist attraction during the summer of 1938 with excursion vessels carrying passengers out of Boston Harbor. A fall storm finished the hull which sank. After this, Graves ledge was renamed "Salisbury Pinnacle." *Photo courtesy of the Peabody Museum of Salem.*

On April 22, 1938, the steamer *City of Salisbury* was entering Boston harbor in dense fog when she was impaled on an "uncharted rock" on Graves Ledge. The ship was inbound from Calcutta, India and had a cargo of exotic wild animals aboard. Some of the creatures were monkeys, trumpet birds, pythons and several deadly cobras. The ship was hard aground, and the wave action was grinding away at the hull. Ominous groans of the tearing steel plates echoed throughout the hull as the swells tipped the ship back and forth like a pendulum. The animals were removed, but a portion of the rest of the cargo was lost. The ship broke in half and disappeared a few months later. Arthur Gaskill, a Boston motion picture news photographer for Hearst Metrotone News went aboard the zoo ship and related his experience:

"As we went up the gang plank the sound of the animals was very evident, I expected to be challenged by some member of the crew, but no one bothered us. Members of the crew walking by paid us no heed, and when I spoke to a couple of them they merely shook their heads and kept going about their business. A reporter in our group told me that there wasn't anyone on deck who spoke English.

So . . Great . . I went about shooting pictures, cages of animals on deck, even a couple of monkeys that were running loose up and down the rigging. Then I figured I needed a semi-high shot, just off the deck for a better all encompassing angle. And there it was, a long wicker-type chest, about 15 feet long, and about four feet off the deck, as I climbed on top of it I noticed that the top was hinged, and was secured by a bent wire thru a metal hasp like a padlock, and I thought at the time, 'that's a flimsy arrangement,' the wire was not even bent over, but just hung there straight across. 'There can't be anything inside'. . . So I went about making various shots with different lenses, and was quite pleased with the angle, showing the whole deck, cages, crew members, and the monkeys again. Just about the time I thought I had finished with this angle, the only member of the crew, the first mate, [so I learned afterwards] came up on deck from a hatch, looked at me and said in a calm voice, 'better watch that wire catch, there is a twelve foot Python inside of what you are standing on.' There are ten things I am scared to death of and nine of them are snakes. I was on the track team in high school as a shot-putter . . . but this is one time I broke all records for the standing broad jump . . . I literally flew through the air, landed, running onto the small boat . . I had had it . . . I did manage to make one more long shot of the ship as we pulled away, but the camera was shaky."

Above: The steamer *Malamton* out of Jacksonville, Florida for Boston with a cargo of lumber ran ashore on the southeast point of Block Island near the lighthouse. The accident occurred on April 26, 1938, and holed the hull with her bow on the rocks. Two weeks later the ship was refloated and towed to New York for repairs. **Below:** On August 17, 1938, the United States Army Engineers dredge *William T. Rossell* was working in Hog Island channel at midnight when she struck a rock on the starboard side. The rock tore a four foot hole in the hull below the water line near the forward engines, and the ship was grounded to prevent her loss. The ship lay on the side of the channel for a few days while temporary repairs were made. The tug *Resolute* towed her to Boston where she underwent repairs. *Photos courtesy of Paul C. Morris, Nantucket, Massachusetts.*

On September 21, 1938, a hurricane roared into New England centered at the state of Rhode Island. Before the storm was over, 600 persons died and property damage was placed at three hundred million dollars. Entire communities were wiped out. The entire waterfront area of the state along with ships, boats, docks and piers was devastated. All communications were severed completely. It was weeks before normal services could be resumed.

Above: During the hurricane and tidal wave the water level in Providence was at a new high. Sue Ewen stands beside the brass plaques on the wall of the historic Old Market House in Market Square. The new record - 13 feet 8½ inches above mean high water at the height of the storm. *Photo by William H. Ewen, Jr., Providence, Rhode Island.* Below: The great hurricane and tidal wave of September 21, 1938, devastated shipping all along the Rhode Island coastline. The Newport-Jamestown ferry *Governor Carr* was driven ashore at Jamestown by the high winds and waves. *Photo courtesy of the Mariners Museum, Newport News, Virginia.*

The Fall River line freighter *New Haven* was tossed up on the shore by the storm. *Photo courtesy of the Mariners Museum, Newport News, Virginia.*

Above: The tanker *Phoenix* with 57,000 gallons of gasoline was anchored in the Taunton River. The storm carried it, with both anchors dragging, five miles up the river where it finally grounded high on the shore at Somerset, Mass. **Below:** The summer excursion steamer *Monhegan* sank at her slip off Dyer Street in Providence, Rhode Island. One of her life boats was carried away by the storm and was found in the doorway of a restaurant, four blocks away. *Photos by R. Loren Graham, courtesy of Steamship Historical Society of America.*

Above: In the 1930's a larger more modern vessel served as the Coast Guard's City Point Station in Dorchester Bay near Boston, Massachusetts. The station was discontinued during World War II. **Below:** Another veteran steamer down at the dock due to old age. After nearly fifty years steaming in Penobscot Bay down Maine the *Vinalhaven* sank at the pier in Rockland, Maine, in November, 1938. She was raised, and the metal parts sold for scrap and the wooden hull cast away to rot on Monroe Island Bar in the Mussel Ridge Channel. *Photo from the Marine collection of Frank E. Claes, Orland, Maine.*

The Texaco tanker *Lightburne* ran aground on February 10, 1939, in dense fog on the southeast end of Block Island with 72,000 barrels of gasoline and kerosene aboard. The grounding caused hull damage, and the vessel filled and sank by the stern. Salvage operations were undertaken and some of the petroleum removed, but winter storms halted work and the tanker broke up and was a total loss. *Photos courtesy of Paul C. Morris, Nantucket, Massachusetts.*

Above: On the morning of May 24, 1939, the United States Navy submarine *Squalus* sank while on a routine training dive off the coast of New Hampshire. Later that afternoon the sub tender *Falcon* arrived on the scene and prepared to send divers down. **Below:** On the fantail of the *Falcon* is the rescue bell and a diver being lifted over the side to dive on the sunken submarine. *Photos courtesy of Portland Press Herald, Portland, Maine.*

On May 24, 1939, just after eight in the morning the United States Navy submarine *Squalus* was on a routine training dive off the Isle of Shoals, New Hampshire, when a high speed induction valve stuck open, flooding the aft compartments. The submarine sank in 240 feet of water with fifty-nine men aboard. Thirty-three of the crew were in the forward section. Shortly afterward communications were set up between the sunken vessel and another submarine on the surface. The Navy rushed the submarine tender *Falcon* to the scene, and with divers and a rescue bell they succeeded in bringing these 33 crewmen to the surface on the next day. The other 26 men in the aft section drowned. On September 14, the hull was raised and towed to Portsmouth, New Hampshire. She was repaired and went to sea again.

Above: On May 25, 1939, the diving bell has returned to the surface and survivors of the *Squalus* are helped onto the deck of the *Falcon*. Thirty-three men were saved. **Below:** The bow of the *Squalus* raised out of water for ten seconds on an aborted salvage attempt on July 13th. The sub sank again and was not raised for another month. *Photos courtesy of the Portland Press Herald, Portland, Maine.*

Above: With the passing of years wooden schooners began to rot away in the ship graveyards. A few of them still would sail and they would still get into trouble in storms. The *Thomas H. Lawrence* came ashore on Cranes Beach at Ipswich, Massachusetts, on August 30, 1939 in a storm. The Coast Guard saved the crew of six, but the vessel was hard up on the beach and salvage proved to be difficult. The vessel was finally removed by digging a channel, and then a Coast Guard tug pulled the schooner to deep water. Her days of sailing were almost over, however, as on her next trip south in 1940 she put into the port of New Bedford, and, because of her poor condition, was condemned. *Photo courtesy of the Mariners Museum, Newport News, Virginia.* **Below:** At 3 a.m. on the clear night of September 17, 1939, the 3200 ton Norwegian freighter, *Rio Branco* ran up on the rock ledges of Eastern Point at Gloucester, Cape Ann, Massachusetts. The helmsman mistook Eastern Point Lighthouse for Boston Lighthouse - a twenty mile error. The ship was wedged on the rocks for seven days while salvagers unloaded her cargo to lighten her. She was pulled off and then proceeded to Boston to be drydocked for repairs to the damaged hull. *Photo courtesy of the Peabody Museum of Salem.*

CHAPTER EIGHT

In 1940 the United States' economy began to flourish. The American railroads were carrying more freight than ever before, and exports hit new highs as the war in Europe grew larger. President Roosevelt won a third term in office - which ended a 144 year old tradition in the United States of no more than two terms for presidents. The war in Europe created havoc in the smaller countries as the German Army directed by Adolph Hitler went on a rampage. In June, President Roosevelt declared the existence of a limited national emergency which, in effect, gave the government control over all American and foreign shipping in United States continental waters.

In 1941, the United States adopted the policy of "lend-lease" for the friendly nations in Europe. The rush of cargoes overseas was underway, and again the submarine menace loomed as Germany retaliated. This created another ship shortage. In February 1941, in a report from Rome, the Vatican deplored the practice of the captain going down with his ship. This tradition was tantamount to suicide, which was contrary to Christian principles. In reply, the Italian officers stated that the request would be ignored as traditions took precedent over religious views. The Vatican responded that the men should think of their mothers who implore the men to leave the sinking ship last, but "leave it."

Another tragic submarine accident occurred on June 20, 1941, when the United States Navy sub, 0-9, sank 24 miles off the coast of Maine in 440 feet of water. Parts of the interior insulation of the submarine were picked up on the surface, which confirmed suspicions that the vessel had collapsed. Divers were sent down to inspect the hull, but they encountered breathing problems at the depth of 370 feet and had to return to the surface. The submarine was given up as lost with her crew of 33 men.

In August of 1941, a new automatic signal device for lifeboats was reported in production. It was designed to work at the flick of a switch by anyone in the boat, thus negating the need for a radio man in each lifeboat when a ship sank. The device was perfected to simplify rescue operations during wartime, and it even worked underwater. In addition to the distress signal, the radio would also transmit the latitude and longitude in degrees and minutes.

The *Seguin,* towing a barge up the Kennebec on June 18, 1940, hit a submerged pier at the Richmond Bridge holing her on the starboard side leaving a four-foot gash. She dropped the barge and headed for the Dresden shore where she was beached with only the forward end out of water. The salvage lighter *Sophia* came down from Rockland and a diver patched the hole. She was taken to Portland for permanent repairs and then returned to the Kennebec. *Photo courtesy of the Peabody Museum of Salem.*

Early Sunday morning, August 25, 1940, the Newport trawler *Palestine* came ashore on Long Nook beach in Truro on lower Cape Cod. The cause of the grounding was blamed on a faulty compass. Coast Guardsmen worked for two days and with the aid of the cutters *Harriet Lane* and *Travis* pulled the vessel off the shore into deep water. As usual on Cape Cod, the ship ashore brought hundreds of people out to view the accident. Two artists record the event on canvas.

Above: The steamer *Essex* from Lisbon for New York ran aground on September 25, 1941, at Block Island, Rhode Island. The ship stranded at the same location as the tanker *Lightburne* in 1939 (page 137). The hull of the *Lightburne* is visible ahead of the bow of the *Essex*. **Below:** The ship had 39 tons of general cargo and 600 tons of cork. The hull was damaged, and the ship had sunk on the rocks, and salvage was not possible. **Bottom:** A December storm swept the superstructure off the hull and she went to pieces soon after. *Photos courtesy of the Mariners Museum, Newport News, Virginia.*

Above: On December 10, 1941, the motor vessel *Oregon* was in collision with the United States Navy battleship *New Mexico* 25 miles south of Nantucket. The freighter was hit in the bow and is shown in a Coast Guard photograph down by the bow just prior to sinking. The accident occurred at night as both vessels were observing wartime blackout and were running without lights. Seventeen men were lost from the *Oregon*. The Navy made no announcement about damage or casualties on the battleship. Some of the survivors were brought ashore by the New Bedford fishing trawler *Viking*. **Below:** The Norwegian freighter *Lista* had a fire in the engine room after leaving New York on August 8, 1940. New York fire boats managed to extinguish the blaze and the ship was returned to Staten Island for repairs. *Photo courtesy of the Mariners Museum, Newport News, Virginia.*

Above: On February 9, 1942, at pier 88 in New York City the famous *Normandie,* pride of the French line caught fire as workers were converting her to wartime use. As fire boats poured water on the blaze on the upper three decks, the ship took a port list from the weight of the water. **Opposite:** The result was a capsize and loss of the noted ship. Salvage was attempted but proved too costly. Payment was made to France for the loss, and the *Normandie* went to the scrap yard. *Photos courtesy of the Mariners Museum, Newport News, Virginia.*

In December, 1941, Pearl Harbor in Hawaii was attacked by air and sea forces of the Empire of Japan, and the United States was again embroiled in a world wide conflict. The war brought on shortages and rationing all over the country. After the Pearl Harbor attack, shipping was at a premium. The United States took over the French liner *Normandie* in New York harbor and began converting it to a troopship. The ship was built in 1935 and was the pride of the French line. She was the grandest liner afloat with luxury in her first class accommodations fit for kings and queens. The vessel was of 83,000 gross tons and could speed across the Atlantic at 31 knots. During the conversion a workman's torch ignited a pile of kapok lifejackets, and the fire quickly spread to other parts of the superstructure. New York fireboats pumped over 800,000 gallons of water aboard to fight the blaze, and the ship took a 10 degree list to port. As workmen tried to pump out water from the upper decks the list increased to 17 degrees. Late at night the list increased to 35 degrees, and in the early hours of the next morning the vessel rolled over on her side. This was the end of the *Normandie.* Later she was righted and taken to the scrap yards.

The pleasure schooner went to war in the 1940's. Coast Guard Reserves manned wooden yachts and carried out submarine patrols from the coast of Massachusetts down to New York. *Photo courtesy of the United States Coast Guard, Boston, Massachusetts.*

The war news dominated the headlines in the newspapers and marine casualties were generally censored. Anyone appearing near the harbors or shorelines with a camera was suspected of spy activities; so, few photographs were made except those by official photographers of the armed services. Stark signs of war were visible along the banks of the Cape Cod Canal during this time when torpedo-damaged ships would pass through on their way to shipyards for repairs. Some of the pleasure yachts went to war in New England waters when the Coast Guard took over a fleet of wooden sailing craft and sent them on submarine patrols manned by the Coast Guard Reserves. They sailed in all kinds of weather and stalked the U-boats in the shipping lanes near the coast, and they adopted the name of the "Corsairs." They were equipped with hydrophones to track the subs. If contact was made they would radio headquarters, and planes and surface craft would be dispatched to sink the sub. This would probably be the last time that sailing ships would go to war.

Above: The damage caused by a torpedo is graphically illustrated in this photograph of the tanker *Bidwell* after she was hit on April 6, 1942. Half inch thick steel plate was bent like paper and required many weeks of repairs. *Photo courtesy of the Mariners Museum, Newport News, Virginia.* **Below:** During the war, torpedoed ships were commonplace. On April 16, 1942, a German submarine operating in the Atlantic sank the British merchant ship *Empire Thrush*. A Coast Guard patrol plane made this shot as the ship went under. *Photo courtesy of the United States Coast Guard.*

On June 28, 1942, the collier *Stephen R. Jones* struck the rocky bank of the Cape Cod Canal near the Bourne Bridge. The damage incurred caused the ship, with a cargo of 7,149 tons of coal, to sink by the head. When the tide changed in the canal the vessel swung around and hit the opposite bank, tearing her steel plates in the stern, and she sank broadside in the canal completely blocking traffic in the middle of World War II. It took engineers 28 days to blow up the wreck and clear the waterway for traffic. *Photo courtesy of Army Corps of Engineers.*

In Newport, Rhode Island on April 10, 1942, one would have thought that the Navy had gone to war in homewaters when a short circuit in a safety switch accidently fired a motor torpedo from a P.T. boat on practice runs. The underwater missile ran wild for about six miles in Narragansett Bay and then struck the Navy cargo vessel *Capella* and injured eight crewmen. The explosion shook houses along the shoreline, and the *Capella* started to sink. Navy tugs pushed the freighter to shoal water where she settled by the stern. During the war, many odd accidents occurred to the men in the Navy. Destroyers stationed on the North Atlantic encountered high seas most of the time, and it was rugged duty. In May of 1943, a big wave broke over a destroyer and swept a seaman off the after deck house into the ocean. A life ring was tossed to him by a shipmate, but he was soon lost in the high seas and could not be found. 40 minutes later, he was getting tired and cold when another destroyer came along and the seaman was taken by a big wave and deposited on the new destroyer's fantail - and he lived to tell this tale.

Early in the war the Coast Guard acquired a new machine. The helicopter seemed a natural tool for the types of rescues performed by the modern lifesavers. One of the first practical uses came in 1944 when Commander Frank A. Erickson ferried some cases of blood plasma from New York to Sandy Hook, New Jersey, to assist medics in treating men wounded in a destroyer explosion outside New York harbor. In May, 1944, heavy fog caused a collision among five ships outside New York harbor. Four Liberty ships and a tanker were involved but, luckily, there were no injuries to crewmen and no fire developed. The collision occurred near the Ambrose lightship, about five miles from shore.

On October 26, 1943, the cargo ship *James Longstreet* grounded on Sandy Hook, New Jersey in gale winds during a flood tide. She was one of three ships that grounded that night and were trapped in the sands. *The above photo was made by Burke Maloney of the Asbury Park Press.* There were no injuries to the crew; but the hull was badly damaged. The ship lay on the sands for a month while repairs were made to the hull. She was refloated on November 23rd and towed to New York where further repairs were made. She was however, declared a total loss because of the damage and was used as a test ship in various projects by the Navy and later towed to Cape Cod Bay and grounded off Eastham to be used as a target ship for the various aerial arms of the military in New England. The photo below by the author shows the ship as it appeared in 1978 after thirty odd years of being bombed, hit, and missed by our boys on training missions. It is fairly obvious that they could hit the middle but were not too sharp on the ends In 1978, Noel W. Beyle of Eastham wrote a narrative of hysterical history and fabulous folklore about the old Liberty Ship and her mis-adventures on the anniversary of her arrival in Cape Cod Bay. The book contains numerous photographs of the old ship in various stages of falling apart while being shot at, bombed, and missed in the thirty years in Cape Cod Bay.

On September 14, 1944 a hurricane hit southeastern New England. Property damage was heavy all along the coastline. The Woods Hole Oceanographic Institute's ketch *Atlantis* was blown ashore at Penzance Point in Woods Hole. The picturesque vessel was later refloated. *Photos courtesy of the Woods Hole Oceanographic Institure, Woods Hole, Massachusetts.*

On September 14, 1944, another hurricane hit the east coast of the United States going through southern New England and causing a loss of 100 million dollars in property damage. Remembering the 1938 storm and because of adequate warnings by newspapers and radio, only 31 deaths were recorded - 12 of those were aboard the Vineyard lightship, stationed off Cuttyhunk Island, Massachusetts. The ship sank with all hands in the terrible storm.

Peace returned to the world in 1945. In May, Germany surrendered, and the guns fell silent in Europe. In August the United States unleashed a secret weapon to end the war in the Pacific. The atomic bombs destroyed two Japanese cities and most of their inhabitants. Japan surrendered a few days later.

The Coast Guard was utilizing the helicopter more and more in their rescue missions out over the water. The success of these rotary-wing aircraft was remarkable. In September, 1945, a Navy doctor was flown from Floyd Bennett field in New York harbor to Ambrose Channel and then lowered into a Coast Guard boat to treat an injured fisherman. The man had mangled his arm on a winch aboard the fishing vessel and was in shock and suffering from loss of blood. He was treated on board the Coast Guard boat and then removed to a hospital where he recovered. Treatment of injured persons off shore used to require many hours because of water transportation for the medical personnel. This time factor was reduced to minutes because of the new helicopter lifts. Down through the years, this machine has become an indispensable tool in Coast Guard "search and rescue" operations.

On February 11, 1944, the British steamship *Empire Knight,* 7,244 tons, on her way from St. John, N.B., to New York City missed a buoy off the coast of Maine and ran up on Boon Island Ledge. A northeast storm was blowing a gale and the bow of the freighter was hard up on the ledge while the stern was tossed around by the high seas. An SOS was radioed, and Coast Guard and Navy units rushed to the scene. However, on scene, rescue was next to impossible because of the mountainous seas. The next morning the ship broke in half and the stern section sank almost immediately. Men and boats were tossed into the sea and the final count was 20 saved and 24 lost. Eventually the bow was smashed by the seas and sank. *Photo by the United States Navy, courtesy of the National Archives, Washington, D.C.*

In addition to the helicopter, World War II brought out many other inventions. One valuable addition was radar. Primarily designed to detect enemy aircraft in wartime, it was adapted to surface ships to enable them to navigate in fog, storms, and on dark nights. The electronic eye was a proven aid to navigation and supposedly would eliminate collisions on the high seas. Later developments have placed radar in aircraft for safety in the air and on landings. On December 23, 1946, the Coast Guard was searching by air and sea for an explosive mine reported floating off Cape Cod. The collier *Berwindvale* sighted the mine about 12 miles east of Block Island, Rhode Island, near a channel leading to Providence. Hours later, the New Bedford fishing vessel *Viking* reported a mine about 18 miles northwest of the Nantucket lightship. Both reports led authorities to believe that it was the same mine, but it was never found.

The post war period brought on more problems for the United States. There were labor disputes all over the country which affected all businesses. Labor won high wages for the workers, and the resulting higher prices aided the spiraling inflation. Industry was in a bind, shifting from all-out wartime to limited peacetime production. Immediately following the war, consumers wanted new cars, appliances, and other goods that were not yet available. The Marshall plan for European recovery poured billions into overseas trading, and the shipping industry prospered again. In the latter part of the decade the dark clouds of war were again forming in the Far East, and the 1950's would see the United States again sending men overseas.

Above: On the night of March 3, 1947, the 5,284 ton collier *Oakey L. Alexander* with 8,200 tons of coal on board was battling gale winds, high seas, and a snow storm outside Portland, Maine, when the seas ripped 150-feet off her bow. Fortunately the 32-man crew was located in the after section of the ship. Captain Raymond Lewis managed to beach the crippled ship on the rocky shore of Cape Elizabeth. *Photo courtesy of the United States Coast Guard, Washington, D.C.* **Below:** The Coast Guard set up the breeches buoy and brought all 32 men ashore safely. Other units of the Coast Guard stood by in case they were needed. The hull was a total loss. *Photo by Gardner Roberts, Portland Press Herald, Portland, Maine.*

The Liberty ship *Charles Tufts* climbed up on the breakwater at Sea Gate, Coney Island, New York, on April 25, 1948. The ship with a crew of 24 lay on the rocks until a high tide floated her off with the aid of tugs. *Wide World Photos.*

Above: Shortly after noon on June 27, 1950, in Bay Ridge channel outside New York harbor the *Excalibur* was in collision with the motor ship *Columbia.* Both ships were damaged in the accident. The cause of the accident was a mistake in signals and rudder failure. The weather was clear. The *Excalibur* was beached on Gowanus Flats. She sank by the bow with a 15-foot hole in her port side. There were no injuries. *Photo courtesy of the Mariners Museum, Newport News, Virginia.* **Below:** The old four-masted schooner *Snetind* was a familiar sight aground on Spectacle Island in Boston Harbor from 1936 until 1951. She was a coal and lumber schooner in the 1920's until a fire in her after hold finished her commercial days. She was laid up in Boston in 1928 and remained beside a pier until 1936, when she was towed out into the harbor. A gale drove her ashore on Spectacle Island, and she lay there until July 1951, and was then towed out to deep water off Boston Light and scuttled. *Photo courtesy of the Peabody Museum of Salem.*

CHAPTER NINE

In January, 1950, the population of the United States had risen to 150 million people. In Boston, a gang of robbers stole $2,775,395 from the security firm of Brinks, Inc. On the international front, the United States and Russia were engaged in a cold war of words, ideas, and propaganda. In June, war flared up in Korea, and American troops were sent as part of a United Nations peace-keeping force. In this country, the popularity of television spurred a phenomenal expansion of an industry presenting pictures of entertainment, news, and sports in one's own home, which brought a marked social change in the nation.

At sea, on January 13, 1950, the Ambrose lightship was sideswiped in the fog by an unidentified vessel which carried away her spare anchor and damaged the radio antenna. Again in March, the lightship was hit in the fog when the Grace Line ship *Santa Monica* rammed into the starboard side of the battered light vessel. The lightship was towed into New York for repairs by the cutter *Mariposa*. Early in 1950 the Navy announced new developments in the field of sonar. The instrument could then be tuned in to hear fish swimming. The electronic listening device was perfected to locate enemy submarines during the war. The latest innovations included echo soundings on a printed chart which would aid in locating schools of fish, or even shipwrecks on the bottom of the ocean.

The Plimsoll mark is a series of load lines on the sides of ocean going ships indicating the depth to which the vessel can be loaded in different trades relative to prevailing weather in various zones. There is one mark, WNA, specially designed for one area in the world: Winter in the North Atlantic. This ocean is a confusion of weather - like a witch, brewing up gales and storms in a caldron. Storms born off Newfoundland grow from a gale to a full hurricane with nothing in their path but open sea and vulnerable ships. The winter of 1951-52 seemed to be one continuous storm on the North Atlantic, and scores of ships were broken down at sea; salvage tugs steaming 24-hours a day could not keep up with the incessant demands for their services. There were fatal accidents, collisions, explosions and blinding blizzards. There were 100 m.p.h. winds and 70-foot waves - and it seemed, if you read the newspapers, that only one man fought the seas.

This episode occurred aboard the United States freighter *Flying Enterprise*. A storm had caused her cargo to shift and with her holds flooded, she developed a 50-degree list. Captain Kurt Carlsen ordered the crew to abandon ship, but he remained aboard to try to save her. For two weeks, the story of this man trying to save his ship was headlined in almost every newspaper in the world. A British tug (aptly named *Turmoil*) took the *Flying Enterprise* in tow. A crewman from the tug, Kenneth R. Dancy, joined Capt. Carlsen aboard the crippled ship, and for ten storm-tossed days they fought a battle against the North Atlantic. The sea finally won after the towline broke 50 miles south of the British Isles and the ship was lost but both men were saved. Captain Carlsen was decorated for keeping up the traditions of the sea.

Above: On February 18, 1952, two tankers, the *SS Pendleton* and the *SS Fort Mercer* broke in two the same day, 40 miles apart, in a blizzard with 70 m.p.h. winds and 60-foot seas off the coast of Cape Cod, Massachusetts. The bow section of the *Pendleton* was saved and towed into port. The stern section grounded off Monomoy Island. **Below:** The bow section of the *Fort Mercer* was judged to be a menace to navigation and was sunk by Coast Guard gunfire. Seventy men were saved and fourteen were lost from the accidents of the two tankers. *Photos courtesy of the United States Coast Guard, Washington, D.C.*

Above: The *City of New York,* Admiral Richard Byrd's flagship, used on the first Antarctic expedition in the 1920's. In the 1940's she was converted to a cargo schooner and sailed out of Nova Scotia. **Below:** On December 30, 1952, the ship went aground off Yarmouth, Nova Scotia, and caught fire. The crew was rescued by a patrol boat. The ship was a total loss. *Photos courtesy of the Mariners Museum, Newport News, Virginia.*

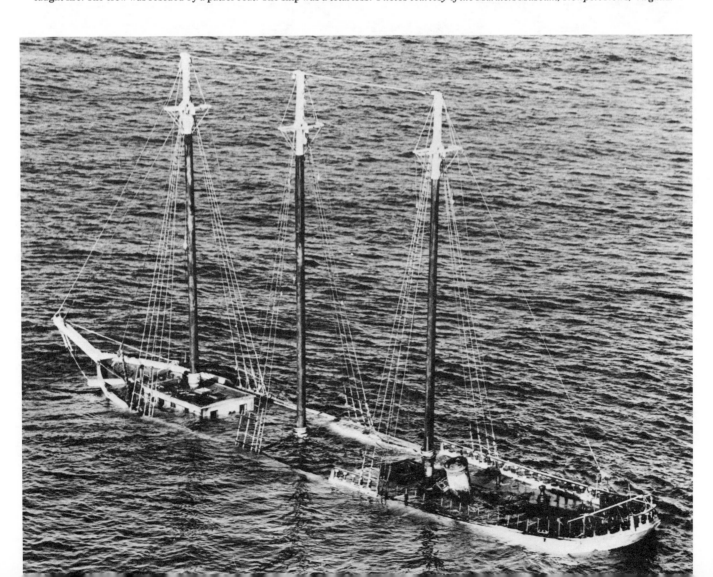

The storms continued into March, and the Liberty ship *Rachel Jackson* limped into New York harbor with her captain, William R. Thomas, directing his ship from the sick bay. A storm-lashed sea had smashed the bridge and its captain. It had broken his leg, fractured his ribs, and had left him with multiple cuts and bruises. In June, 1952, a collision at sea off Cape Cod in clear weather brought the 10,000 ton tanker *Esso Chattanooga* against the Gloucester fishing vessel *Albatros.* The surviving fishermen said that their captain, Bjorguin Einarsson gave up his life rather than risk overcrowding a dory with twelve shipmates already aboard. On December 2, 1955, the Gloucester fishing vessel *Veronica N.* was afire and her captain, Eugene M. Naves, drove her aground off Good Harbor beach. Firefighters could not reach the boat but a Coast Guard helicopter carried a hose from the fire truck on the beach out to the crew of the burning boat and they extinguished the flames in the fo'c's'le and saved their vessel.

On February 16, 1953, two Coast Guard boatmen froze to death on a breakwater outside Saybrook, Connecticut, harbor. The men had been stranded when the engine of their launch failed and high winds had carried them against the jetty. In July, 1953, the Korean war ended, and a truce was signed. On October 16, an explosion and fire killed 36 men and injured 40 aboard the aircraft carrier, *Leyte,* while in Boston Navy Yard for an overhaul. Cause of the blast was unknown, and sabotage was suspected. On September 14 the *SS Hawaiian* was heading west out of the Cape Cod Canal on a foggy night. At the Cleveland Ledge light station, in the center of Buzzards Bay, fog signals were being sounded and the *Hawaiian* loomed out of the mist and nearly hit the station head on. The captain said that he thought the light was another ship. The ship's helm was put over at the last moment and missed the light by about 10 yards, taking two buoys with her bow.

What the hell do you mean "rules of the road," this is the Cleveland Ledge Lighthouse!

The *Pilgrim Belle* ran aground in the fog on Spectacle Island in Boston harbor on June 22, 1955. The 272 passengers were removed by small craft and the vessel was eventually refloated to finish out the summer season. *Photo courtesy of the Mariners Museum, Newport News, Virginia.*

The 441 foot Italian freighter *Etrusco* went ashore at Scituate, Massachusetts on the night of March 16, 1956, during an old fashioned New England nor'easter with snow and wind that forced cancellation of Boston's St. Patrick's day parade. The crew was taken off the ship by the Coast Guard using the old breeches buoy. Later the freighter became a tourist attraction at the seashore town as she remained on the beach for eight months. She was pulled off on Thanksgiving day by the Global Shipping Company who renamed the freighter *Scituate*. *Photo courtesy of the United States Coast Guard.*

On January 11, 1954, three Boston Harbor Pilots were drowned as they were boarding a tanker outside the harbor. A towering wave swamped the dory they were in, dumping them in the icy waters. One of the worst peacetime disasters in the United States Navy occurred on May 26, 1954. Explosions and a fire in the catapult room, killed over 100 men and injured 200 more aboard the aircraft carrier *Bennington,* while she was on maneuvers in the Atlantic Ocean, about 75 miles south of Newport, Rhode Island.

In the early days, the Life Saving Service closed their stations every summer during the months of June and July. In the 1950's the Coast Guard was doing just the opposite, in that they reactivated stations that had been closed for the winter months, all along the east coast. The summer boating season adds more work to the Coast Guard function and keeps the men busy. Extra boats are utilized to help prevent accidents. In 1954, Congress voted funds to complete the United States section of the St. Lawrence Seaway. The waterway provided access for larger ocean going ships to visit the Great Lakes ports. The 182 mile seaway was completed and opened in 1959.

Early in the morning of July 7, 1955, a tugboat off the mouth of Chesapeake Bay picked up a "mayday" on the radiotelephone. The message was from the vessel *Blue Star* stating that she had struck a log and was sinking, 55 miles southeast of New York City. The message was relayed to the Coast Guard, who launched planes and directed cutters to the scene. The messages continued . . . 'the vessel's 21 passengers were in the water without any lifejackets' . . .the voice then faded, and was lost. Aircraft and rescue ships searched all day and the following night, but nothing was found at the location given in the radio message. The next day, two Long Island youths were picked up, and they confessed to the hoax. They had broken into a fishing vessel on Long Island and had used the radiotelephone to broadcast the fake emergency. The young men had been drinking prior to the incident - which cost the taxpayers $100,000 for the search. They were prosecuted and convicted in the Federal Court.

Above: Late at night on July 25, 1956, in dense fog the *Andrea Doria* was struck on the starboard side just under the bridge by the *Stockholm.* This photo was made about 8 in the morning as the 29,082-ton Italian liner is taking on water and has been abandoned by her crew. **Below:** A helicopter removed one of the injured from the stern of the Swedish liner *Stockholm.* 52 persons died as a result of the collision. *Photos courtesy of the United States Coast Guard.*

Late in the evening of July 25, 1956, the *Andrea Doria*, queen of the Italian line, was steaming towards New York City, fifty miles south of Nantucket Island in a heavy wet fog. A few miles west, heading east was the Swedish motor vessel *Stockholm.* She had left New York that day and was approaching the Nantucket lightship. Just after 11 p.m. the *Stockholm* collided with the *Andrea Doria* and knifed a third of the way through the side of the Italian liner. The S O S brought scores of ships to the scene. The rescue effort was huge. Sixteen-hundred and sixty-two persons were saved and only fifty-two died, these being the result of the collision. The next morning, at 10:09 a.m., the *Andrea Doria* turned over and sank in 225 feet of water, where she rests to this day. Modern vessels depend heavily on their radar in fog to hold speed and maintain schedules. The chief cause of the accident was attributed to careless and negligent operation of the radar and the handling of the ships in the fog. It was observed afterwards, ironically, that had the ships not been equipped with radar, the accident probably would not have happened.

163

Above: The 656-foot Italian liner *Andrea Doria* in the last stages of sinking as her funnel touches the water and an empty lifeboat drifts aimlessly away. **Below:** The ship begins her final plunge to the bottom in 225 feet of water. *Photos courtesy of the United States Coast Guard, Washington, D.C.*

Above: In dense fog, on the night of July 23, 1956, outside New York harbor, the American freighter *Fairisle* collided with the Panamanian tanker *San Jose II*. The freighter received a large hole in her port side amidships. Passengers and crew were picked up by the Coast Guard, and the ship turned over on her starboard side and settled in Gravesend Bay. The *Fairisle* was refloated six months later. *Photo courtesy of the Mariners Museum, Newport News, Virginia.* **Below:** The 422 foot collier *Reading* loaded with 10,000 tons of coal ran onto Henrietta Rock off New Bedford on February 18, 1957. The rock cracked the hull and the *Reading* was impaled on the reef until she was unloaded by salvage crews. *Photo by William P. Quinn.*

Above: On December 3, 1956 a 7½ million dollar fire gutted the Luckenbach Pier at 35th Street, Brooklyn, New York City. Tugboats from the Moran Towing and Transportation Company assisted five freighters moored at the pier away from the flames. *New York Daily News photo.*

On December 3, 1956, a fire and explosion destroyed the Luckenbach pier, 35th Street in Brooklyn, New York. Ten persons were killed, and over two-hundred and fifty people were injured, and damage was estimated at seven and one half million dollars. The fire started in mid afternoon, and Brooklyn firefighters were working the fire when a huge explosion occurred in the center section of the pier. Several types of inflamable goods were stored on the dock, including seven tons of explosives. Soon after the fire began, tugboats from all over the harbor arrived to assist the five ships moored in the area adjacent to the pier to escape the flames. All were moved successfully to other moorings. The fire burned for two days.

On October 4, 1958, transatlantic jet service began between New York and London. The effect was not immediate, but passenger traffic aboard ships dropped steadily in the 1960's. It was evident that the jet aircraft would replace ocean liners, it was just a question of time. In other news of the 1950's, United States exports averaged fifty billion dollars per year, providing a heavy flow of ship traffic in the sea lanes around New England. Hawaii and Alaska joined with the other states to bring the number to fifty. Congress created the National Aeronautics and Space Agency for the exploration of outer space. America was getting ready to enter the space age of the 1960's.

Above: The Norwegian freighter *Belleville* went on the rocks off Brenton Point, Rhode Island, on September 24, 1957. The ship was bound from Boston to Philadelphia in clear weather when the mishap occurred. Cause of the grounding was listed as a mistake in navigation. **Below:** The ship was hard aground with her bow section floating and rough weather took its toll and the vessel soon split in two pieces. *Photos by John T. Hopf, Newport, Rhode Island.*

Above: The *Belleville* in the final stages. Part of the cargo was recovered. **Below:** A collision in the early morning fog just outside of Newport Harbor took seventeen lives and injured thirty-six. On the morning of August 7, 1958, the *S S Gulfoil,* in ballast, was headed out of Newport, Rhode Island, harbor when she hit the *M V Graham* on the port side forward. The *Graham* had five million gallons of gasoline aboard and burst into flames immediately. *Photos by John T. Hopf, Newport, Rhode Island.*

Above: Flames engulfed both ships as small craft, tugs, and planes from the Coast Guard and Navy bases in the area rushed to the scene. The fire burned for five hours before it was brought under control. **Below:** After the fire was put out aboard the *Gulfoil*, she was beached nearby. Later she was rebuilt. *Photos by John T. Hopf, Newport, Rhode Island.*

Above: In the East River of New York, the tanker *Empress Bay* sank under the Manhattan bridge on June 25, 1958, after she collided with the Swedish freighter *Nebraska* in the early morning hours. Two tanker crewmen were lost, and 49 people were saved. There was 280,000 gallons of gasoline aboard the tanker, which ignited on impact and spread a blanket of fire that engulfed both vessels and adjacent waters, endangering waterfront areas on Manhattan and Brooklyn sides of the river as well as the bridge. The tanker was later raised by commercial salvage operations on September 9, 1958. **Below:** The 135-foot bow section of the Norwegian tanker *Jalanta,* ripped off in a collision with the American liner *Constitution* on March 1, 1959. *Photos courtesy of the United States Coast Guard, Washington, D.C.*

Above: On March 1, 1959, the American luxury liner *Constitution* was in a collision with the Norwegian tanker *Jalanta* in dense fog near the entrance to New York harbor. The tanker was cut in two, and the liner suffered bow damage but there were no injuries. **Below:** Deep patches of steel were gouged out of the port side of the liner *Constitution* in the accident. *Photos courtesy of the United States Coast Guard, Washington, D.C.*

One of the oddest photographs encountered in the search for wreck pictures was this one which was the result of a collision, south of New York City in the Atlantic when the American passenger liner *Santa Rosa* rammed the stern of the American tanker *Valchem* on March 26, 1959. The liner plunged deep into the tanker and took the stack and engine room ventilators away on her bow. One man on the tanker was killed, three were missing and presumed lost, sixteen were injured. There were no injuries on the liner. *Photo courtesy of the United States Coast Guard, Washington, D.C.*

CHAPTER TEN

In the early 1960's the economic outlook was promising as President John F. Kennedy ushered in the "New Frontier." Americans were being launched into space and Colonel John Glenn orbited the earth in 1962. The new containerized cargo ships began arriving in New England ports. A proposal to connect the St. Lawrence River with the Hudson River through Lake Champlain was discussed and favored by marine interests and, although it was a good idea, the costs far outweighed the benefits; so the plan was dropped. A new problem came up in New York City. The Federal Aviation Agency and the United States Army Engineer District employees found that steamships and airliners were in danger of collisions in the Riker's Island Channel. The tall masts were traversing an area in the channel where airliners flew their landing approach to LaGuardia Field thus creating the possibility of a disaster. The problem was solved when the Port of New York set up telephone connections between the Harbor Carriers and the control tower at LaGuardia Field for ship and plane clearance in the danger area.

On June 24, 1960, the freighter *Green Bay* outbound from New York City to East Africa, rammed a relief lightship at the Ambrose station in dense fog. The regular light vessel was at Staten Island for her annual overhaul. The crew of nine quickly put over a rubber raft. The light vessel's lifeboat was damaged in the collision, and the ship sank in ten minutes. The men paddled the raft by hand to move quickly away from their sinking vessel lest they be carried down with her. The Ambrose Channel vessel had suffered numerous accidents in the past. It is situated in a peak traffic area and was named for the man who developed modern New York harbor, John Wolfe Ambrose.

Accidents to aircraft carriers continued to plague the United States Navy as on December 19, 1960, the *U.S.S. Constellation* was swept by fire while still under construction at the Brooklyn Navy Yard. Fifty workers were killed, and one hundred fifty more injured out of the 4,000 man work force aboard. The 10-alarm fire began at 10:30 a.m. when a work vehicle on the hanger deck accidently knocked a valve off a fuel tank. The volatile liquid flowed down a bomb elevator and come in contact with a welder at work. The New York firefighters brought the blaze under control ten hours later, and the damage was estimated at 75 million dollars.

173

Above: On February 21, 1960, the *Monica Smith* of the Swedish-Chicago line was riding out gale winds off Cape Cod when she was driven ashore a mile north of New Beach in Provincetown. It was Washington's birthday weekend, and thousands came to Cape Cod and walked a mile down the beach to see the grounded freighter as witnessed by the many footprints in the sand. She was pulled free a week later without damage. *Photo by William P. Quinn.* **Below:** The 441-foot freighter *Marine Merchant* broke in half just forward of the bridge while battling mountainous seas in a northeast storm in the Gulf of Maine on April 14, 1961. The crew abandoned the vessel early in the morning and were picked up by other merchant ships answering the SOS. The freighter sank at about 10 a.m. Cause of the accident was attributed to improper loading of a bulk sulpher cargo. *Photo courtesy of the United States Coast Guard, Washington, D.C.*

174

Above: The four million dollar dredge *Cartagena* broke away from her tug on December 25, 1961, while some 200 miles off Cape Cod during stormy seas and 70-knot winds. The dredge was being towed from Detroit, Michigan, to Baltimore, Maryland. **Below:** The Coast Guard cutter *Acushnet* passed close-by the drifting dredge as her crew of ten watched rescue so near, yet so far away. A life raft was tossed over and taken aboard the dredge to effect the rescue of the stranded men. *Photos courtesy of the United States Coast Guard, Washington, D.C.*

The life raft with ten survivors from the dredge was pulled to the cutter. One man fell overboard and nearly drowned but was saved by Coast Guardsmen from the *Acushnet* and revived by mouth to mouth resuscitation. The Canadian tug *Foundation Vigilant* secured a line aboard the dredge when the weather abated and towed it to Baltimore. *Photo courtesy of the United States Coast Guard, Washington, D.C.*

Above: Sheathed in ice, the 87-foot dragger *Katie D.* lies grounded on Rocky Neck at Gloucester, Mass. on December 31, 1962. The vessel lost power and drifted ashore in a severe winter storm. Eight Gloucester fishermen were rescued by the Coast Guard. **Below:** On March 19, 1963, the famous former Coast Guard cutter *Bear* sank in the Atlantic 90 miles south of Cape Sable, Nova Scotia. The ninety year old ship, noted for her polar expeditions and rescues, was being towed to Philadelphia to become a museum and restaurant. The towline parted from the tug *Irving Birch,* the foremast collapsed, and the old vessel went to the bottom. *Photos courtesy of the United States Coast Guard, Washington, D.C.*

On March 19, 1963, the final chapter in a ninety year saga of the sea was written eighty miles south of Cape Sable, Nova Scotia, when the noted Coast Guard cutter *Bear* sank. The ship, while under the Coast Guard, had worked the Bering Sea and Arctic waters for almost thirty years and had rescued hundreds of men. She had seen two eras of ships, sail and steam and was rigged for both. She also served Admiral Richard E. Byrd in 1933 on his second Antarctic expedition. Built as a three-masted barkentine in 1873, with an auxiliary steam engine, she had had an illustrious career. Famous for her polar exploits, her future was to have been as an historic museum and restaurant in Philadelphia. She was being towed there when heavy weather parted her towline and the foremast collapsed, and then the seas claimed her. Slowly she slipped under the North Atlantic to her last station.

Above: The United States Navy Minesweeper *Grouse* ran aground on Little Salvage Reef, a rocky ledge about two miles off Rockport, Massachusetts, at 1:15 a.m. on September 21, 1963. Eleven crewmen were taken off by the Coast Guard when heavy seas threatened. *Photo courtesy of the United States Coast Guard.* **Below:** Several refloating tries were made, unsuccessfully. The 136-foot vessel was a total loss and the hull was burned. *Photo courtesy of the Naval Photgraphic Center, Washington, D.C.*

A collision in Buzzards Bay on November 14, 1963, between two vessels using the Cape Cod Canal. The Norwegian freighter *Fernview* collided with the Sun Oil tanker *Dynafuel*. The bow of the freighter was imbedded 20 feet into the portside of the tanker; fire broke out immediately aboard the *Dynafuel* with smoke billowing 250 feet into the air. The tanker was a total loss. *Aerial photo by William P. Quinn.*

The worst submarine disaster in the history of the United States Navy occurred on April 10, 1963, when the nuclear submarine, *Thresher*, sank 220 miles east of Boston, Massachusetts. There were 129 men on board when the vessel submerged while carrying out deep diving tests. Officials said that the hull, which ended 8,400 feet down in the Atlantic, was crushed by the depth. On November 22, 1963, the nation and the world went into mourning when President John F. Kennedy was assasinated in Dallas, Texas. A war hero and the first Roman Catholic President, Kennedy had made significant progress in the civil rights movement and the nation's space program. He was the fourth United States President to be killed in office.

A small miracle occurred in the North Atlantic on Friday the 13th of September, 1963. Franz Strycharczyk, a seaman aboard the West German freighter *Freiburg* fell overboard at night and was lost in the ocean without a life jacket - but he kept on swimming. Fifteen hours later, the man was spotted by the Coast Guard cutter, *Absecon*, 810 miles northeast of Bermuda. He was picked up tired but still alive. A miracle, because the Atlantic Ocean has an area of over thirty-three million square miles.

On August 12, 1966, a Northeast Airlines DC-3 left Nantucket Island at 6:30 p.m. on the regular scheduled flight to Boston. Shortly after take-off the plane had climbed to 3,000 feet when the co-pilot noticed a fishing boat on fire about twelve miles north of the Island. Airline Captain Guy R. Caron radioed Otis Air Force Base about the emergency and dropped down to maintain coverage over the disaster area. The 99-foot New Bedford dragger *Mary and John* burned to the water line and then sank.

The nine man crew had abandoned their ship and were in two lifeboats. The airline crew saw another fishing boat five miles away and the captain wigwagged the liner's wings, an international intercept signal, to guide the scalloper *Charles S. Ashley* to the scene. The crew of the burning boat was picked up by the *Ashley* and returned to New Bedford. The Coast Guard dispatched cutters from Woods Hole but when they arrived at the disaster area the dragger was engulfed in flames. The airliner was thirty-five minutes late arriving in Boston that night.

Above: In late January, 1964, the British supertanker *Federal Monarch* was crippled by a burned out main engine bearing, seventeen miles off Portland, Maine. The tug *Helen B. Moran* passed lines and then towed the huge tanker into Portland harbor for repairs. *Photo by Gardiner Roberts of the Portland Press Herald.* **Below:** On February 19, 1964, the Coast Guard cutter *Coos Bay,* returning from winter patrol on ocean station "Bravo" off Labrador received an SOS from the British motorship *Ambassador,* with a crew of 35. The ship was sinking in the Atlantic 370 miles south of her position. High seas had upset two liferafts on the 18th and 14 crewmen were lost. The *Ambassador* is shown in the photo with her crew in the bow taking a line from the *Coos Bay.* A rescue raft was sent over, and six swimmers from the *Coos Bay* in survival gear assisted the remaining crew members aboard the cutter. *Photo courtesy of the United States Coast Guard.*

In 1958, the Coast Guard entered the computer age and instituted a new rescue program for ships on the North Atlantic. Initial efforts were successful and in the 1960's the operations were expanded to include other ocean areas, and, finally the coverage is now world wide. Dubbed *Amver,* the letters stand for Automated Mutual Assistance Vessel Rescue. It is a merchant vessel plotting program, designed to maintain and provide information on ships for use in "search and rescue" operations. The system is able to forecast the locations of those merchant vessels near an emergency. The computer is told where help is needed and in only moments can identify the names and whereabouts of nearby ships. The rescue center controller handling the case can use this information to radio a suitable vessel that her help is needed. The computer keeps a constant electronic watch on all vessels on the high seas. Ships file periodic position reports to keep the plot accurate. Severe storms are tracked and warnings issued based on weather data from ships at sea by satellite reports. The modern computer had made life at sea much easier.

A noteworthy case occurred on April 24, 1969, in the middle of the Atlantic, when a 24 year old crewman aboard the *MV Tielrode* was stricken with an acute case of appendicitis. The German passenger ship *Bremen*, 158 miles away, was the only ship in the vicinity with a doctor on board. The New York Rescue Coordination Center was apprised of the emergency, and they radioed the Master of the *Bremen,* who immediately changed course and proceeded to a rendezvous point. The next day, the man was transferred to the *Bremen*, was operated on successfully, and recovered fully. A message from New York to the Master: "Your prompt and willing assistance in the emergency medical case was in keeping with the highest tradition of the sea."

On October 16, 1968, the miniature submarine, *Alvin,* operated by the Woods Hole Oceanographic Institute, was lost 120 miles south of Cape Cod and sank to a depth of 4,500 feet. The small research submarine was engaged in deep water operations when a cable parted on board her tender, dropping the sub into the sea with her hatch open. Ten months later, aided by the deep diving sub *Aquanaut,* the *Alvin* was raised and reconditioned and went back into service. On July 20, 1969, America's space program performed its greatest achievement when the lunar vehicle of the Apollo 11 spacecraft landed, and Neil Armstrong became the first man to step on the moon. This was the first of six successful United States Moon landings.

In the 1960's, time caught up with the great ocean liners. The decline in the transatlantic passenger business was caused by the tremendous surge in jet air travel. Shipping companies failed to assess this development correctly in the late 1950's, and efforts to modernize and improve service to re-establish the industry failed. The fares in the air were lower than on board ships, and it required only seven hours to cross in a jetliner. The fate of some of the more noted steamships varied. In September, 1967, the Cunard Line retired the Atlantic "Queens." The *Queen Mary* was converted to a hotel in Long Beach, California, and the *Queen Elizabeth* burned and sank in Hong Kong harbor. In 1969, the *United States,* the fastest and most modern liner, completely air conditioned and fireproof, was laid up in Newport News, Virginia. One of the grandest liners was the *France.* Built in 1960, she was laid up in Le Harve in 1974. In October, 1977, it was announced that the ship had been sold to interests in Saudi Arabia and was to become a hotel in the Middle East. The new *Queen Elizabeth II* began service in 1969. She was designed to cruise the Caribbean in the winter and for transatlantic crossings in the summer. The ship was still engaged on these runs in 1979.

In 1882, an experiment was carried out at the Scottish port of Peterhead. Oil was poured on rough waters at the harbor mouth to smooth out the waves so that a small boat could enter the harbor. The test was successful and oil was used for this purpose at sea and near the shores to put down storm tossed waters in order to rescue shipwrecked mariners. The effect on the environment was not a factor until recently however. Energy, oil spills, and oil shortages all over the world would exacerbate some of the problems of the 1970's.

Above: On March 1, 1964, the Liberian tanker *Amphialos* was battling a North Atlantic storm and heavy seas when the vessel broke in half. The bow section sank and the stern section was taken in tow by the salvage tug *Curb* of the Merritt, Chapman and Scott Company of New York. The remaining part of the ship sank about 250 miles east of Boston. Note the tow line hanging off the stern of the ship. *Photo courtesy of the United States Coast Guard, Boston, Mass.* **Below:** The *Aquanaut II,* caught fire off Plum Island, Massachusetts, on November 2, 1964. Two Coast Guard boats and a Coast Guard helicopter raced to the scene to fight the blaze erupting from an oil burner in the engine room. The vessel was towed into the Merrimac River Station and was not severely damaged. *Photo courtesy of the United States Coast Guard, Washington, D.C.*

182

On April 12, 1966 the Italian luxury liner *Michelangelo,* ran into a monster storm in the Atlantic and was battered by 45 foot waves. The giant waves smashed the liner on her forward section just below the bridge and killed three people and injured eleven. She is shown headed for New York on April 15th. *Photo courtesy of the United States Coast Guard, New York, N.Y.*

At various times in the stormy North Atlantic three or four big waves will combine to form a giant that travels across the ocean and does considerable damage to anything in its path. Proof that these big waves exist is attested to by the crews in the ships that experience them. In January 1910, the liner *Lusitania* was hit by a wave estimated to be eighty feet in height. She was buried under a mountain of water causing damage to the wheel house on the upper bridge. In 1942, a giant wave hit the *Queen Mary* broadside and lay her on her side in the trough with her upper decks awash. Had she gone over a few more inches she would have gone to the bottom and taken 15,000 American soldiers with her. In April of 1966, the Italian liner *Michelangelo* was smashed by a big wave in the North Atlantic which stove in her forward section killing three persons and injuring ten. The 46,000 ton liner arrived in New York City with a big hole in her superstructure under the bridge with her bow crumpled. Captain Giuseppe Soletti said that a mountain fell on the ship, and tons of water crushed the bulkheads into a tangled mass. Two passengers and one crewman were killed. In September, 1978, a violent Atlantic storm with 70 m.p.h. winds enveloped the *Queen Elizabeth II*. Sixty foot waves caused damage to the bow area of the ship. The giant waves are not restricted to the North Atlantic. Reports of them from all over the world support the theory that many ships that suddenly disappear without a trace are struck by these giant walls of water and are driven under the sea.

Above: A Coast Guard helicopter hovers on scene as tugs and fireboats battle the raging fire on board the 546-foot British tanker *MV Alva Cape* after her collision with the 604-foot American tanker *S.S. Texaco Massachusetts*, in the Kill Van Kull between Bayonne, New Jersey, and Staten Island on June 16, 1966. The *Alva Cape* was inbound with 143,000 barrels of naptha, while the *Texaco Massachusetts*, having just offloaded a cargo of oil, was in ballast and outbound. **Below:** Just in time. Crewmen from the sinking fishing vessel *Maureen & Michael* are rescued by a rubber raft in the rough and cold North Atlantic east of Newfoundland. The raft is from the Coast Guard cutter *Castle Rock* which, on her way to the ocean station ''Delta,'' answered the vessel's SOS and saved the crew of eight fishermen and landed them at St. John's Newfoundland. *Photos courtesy of the United States Coast Guard, Washington, D.C.*

Most of the Coast Guard's fifty lightships have been replaced by offshore towers or large navigational buoy's. The Ambrose Lightship station was located at the lower entrance to New York harbor, seven miles east of Sandy Hook, New Jersey. On August 23, 1967, she departed from her station for the last time and her duties were assumed by the New Ambrose offshore tower. *Photo courtesy of the United States Coast Guard, New York, N.Y.*

Above: A stubborn fire burned for more than five hours aboard the British freighter *Manchester Miller* at dockside on the East River in New York City on December 12, 1968. A cargo of chemicals fed the flames and firefighters had to cut holes in the hull to get to the fire. **Below:** The coastal tanker *Mary A. Whalen* ran aground on December 23, 1968, on the jetty at Rockaway Point Breakwater, New York. The vessel had a full load of 150,000 gallons of oil which had to be off loaded to a barge before she could be pulled off on December 26. There was some damage to the tanker but no oil was spilled. *Photos courtesy of the United States Coast Guard, Washington, D.C.*

CHAPTER ELEVEN

In the 1970's widespread attention was focused on the oil tankers, their accidents, and the resulting oil spills. This chapter will cover the subject as a separate entity.

On February 27, 1942, at 12:28 a.m., a Nazi submarine fired two torpedoes into the American oil tanker *R. P. Resor,* 18 miles off the New Jersey coast. The vessel was fully laden with oil. The ship split in half and burned for two days. There were only two survivors. She was the 17th tanker sunk during the first two months of the war. During the hostilities, 1700 tankers were sunk world wide with an estimated loss of seven billion gallons of oil. Some of the oil washed up on the New England shorelines. The cost to the war effort was in millions but the cost of cleaning it up was nothing because at that time the mess was considered a nuisance rather than a disaster.

The damage done by an oil spill on the ocean was not the subject of a much public indignation until March 18, 1967, when the supertanker *Torrey Canyon* grounded and broke in two off Land's End, the southwestern point of the British Isles. Thousands of tons of crude oil fouled the beaches of Cornwall, and hundreds of ocean birds were killed. The oil caused ecological damage measured in the millions of dollars. The spill attracted world wide headlines, which exploited the story for the full effect. After the *Torrey Canyon* disaster, any story about an oil tanker, oil spill or accident received priority treatment by the broadcast and print media. The tanker wrecks seemed to multiply in the ensuing years, as the world demanded more energy, and the oil shippers tried to prolong the use of aging oil tankers beyond their normal longevity in an effort to meet the insatiable demand.

One of the more dangerous tanker accidents involved fire. Two barges collided off Staten Island, New York, in December, 1968. One contained 425,000 gallons of gasoline. There was an explosion, and before the fire was brought under control the beach adjacent to the wreck was in flames. In 1969, at Santa Barbara, California, there was an offshore oil well blow-out that coated the beaches with an estimated three million gallons of crude oil. In December, 1969, the Liberian tanker *Keo* broke in half in the stormy North Atlantic. 210,000 barrels of fuel oil were lost in the ocean, and the ship went down with all hands. Thirty-six men were lost, and the massive search effort turned up only eight bodies.

On February 8, 1970, the 11,379 ton Liberian tanker *Arrow* grounded on Cerberus Rock in Chedabucto Bay in Nova Scotia. The ship broke in half and was a total loss. The crew were all saved, but the oil spilled from the sunken hull fouled the entire bay.

On January 23, 1971, about 385,000 gallons of light fuel spilled into New Haven, Connecticut, harbor when the 23,665-ton tanker *Esso Gettysburg* ran aground. Oil leaked from many holes punctured in the hull and formed a three mile slick in the harbor and in Long Island Sound. There were no injuries to the crew, but a helicopter with a television newsman filming the slick crashed in the sound, injuring the pilot and photographer. The Coast Guard rescued both men.

In 1972, the Coast Guard reported that they had logged four times as many complaints about oil spills as calls from mariners in distress. It was apparent that the public was becoming aware of ecological damage. The people were backed up by the Water Quality Improvement Act of 1970, which required polluters to pay for cleaning up illegal discharges and to pay fines of up to $10,000. In July, 1971, a United States Navy ship spilled 40,000 gallons of oil in New York harbor. In May of 1972, $86,246.41 was paid to the city to cover the cost of cleaning up the waterfronts on Coney Island, Brooklyn, and South Beach, Staten Island.

Above: On March 27, 1967, the Liberian tanker *Torrey Canyon* ran onto Seven Stones Reef off Land's End, England, and became the progenitor of world concern about oil spills. This wreck along with the publicity and the R.A.F. bombing in an attempt to burn the oil, brought to the attention of the world the environmental damage created by oil spills. The thousands of tons of oil that poured from the bowels of the ship blackened Cornwalls summer bathing beaches. *Wide World Photos.* **Below:** On November 6, 1943, a Coast Guard patrol craft stands watch over the burning hull of a torpedoed tanker somewhere off the east coast of the United States. A Navy blimp and other vessels search for the submarine that torpedoed the tanker. This was a common sight at sea during the war. *Photo courtesy of the United States Coast Guard.*

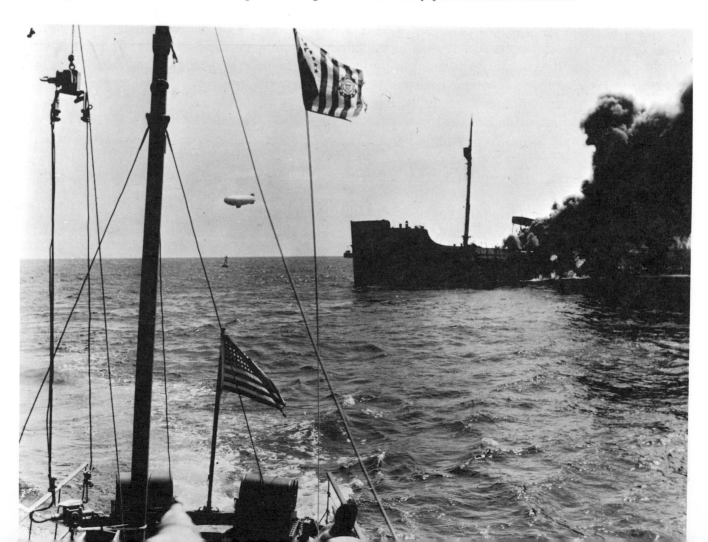

It was at this time that public officials found it politically expedient to attack the shipping companies whenever an accident occurred and the environment was threatened by an oil spill. The beneficial publicity that ensued did much to endear the politician to his constituents, and even more so if the shipwreck happened to occur during or just previous to an election campaign. In April, 1972, in Hartford, Connecticut, Governor Thomas J. Meskill called a news conference to announce "A comprehensive program to protect Long Island Sound and Connecticut's coastline from oil spills." The program included pushing sea lanes farther out in the sound, criminal charges of negligence against masters and pilots, fines for the owners of ships, and recovery of costs for damage and cleanup of the pollution. The Governor added that he was asking the Connecticut Congressional delegation to develop Federal legislation to assist the state in these endeavors.

In October, 1973, a total ban on oil exports to the United States was imposed by the Arabian oil-producing nations right after the outbreak of the Arab-Israeli war. This created shortages, and thus began the long irritating waiting lines at filling stations all over the United States. The shortages caused prices to move rapidly upward, and the export ban was not eased until March in 1974. United States oil companies reported that profits were up between sixty and seventy percent in the last quarter of 1973 over the same period in 1972.

In an effort to economize, oil companies purchased larger tankers to move their cargo. The 200,000 ton supertanker now appeared on the world's oceans. These huge ships did not frequent New England since there is no port deep enough to accommodate them. In 1974, a book about the vessels called *Supership* by Noel Mostert, outlined the shortcomings of these vessels and the ecological dangers that they posed. The oil companies accused the book as being melodramatic and effective propaganda, but the accidents of some of the giant ships since the book was printed have proven that the warnings put forth by Mostert were not without merit.

There were also incidents of explosions in empty tankers. A study reported by the Coast Guard in August, 1974, showed that recent explosions in bulk carriers were the result of slack tanks with ballast water sloshing around and induced by wave motions to generate an electrically charged mist. The oily water being thrown around produced sparks, and an explosion resulted from the static electricity. In January, 1975, the Coast Guard warned residents of coastal areas from Delaware to Rhode Island to watch for sealed steel barrels that might wash ashore. The barrels, painted gray with yellow letters, contained fumes of tetraethel lead, the anti-knock compound, and they might explode. Moreover, the vapors could poison anyone who might inhale them. These drums had been washed overboard from a ship during a storm.

The accidents continued. On January 31, 1975, a collision at Marcus Hook, Pa. caused several explosions aboard the 54,000 ton Liberian tanker *Corinthos*. Local, commercial and Coast Guard firefighters battled the fire for 12 hours before bringing it under control, and 26 persons died in the blazing wreck. The rash of fires brought additional safety regulations. More spills occurred in 1976; on January 1st, a barge rammed the Tappan Zee bridge on the Hudson River and spilled 100,000 gallons of oil. On June 24th, a barge ran aground in the St. Lawrence Seaway at Alexandria Bay and spilled more than 300,000 gallons of bunker oil, threatening wildlife and the resort areas of the Thousand Islands. The cleanup required many weeks of work.

Above: In July, 1972, the Norwegian tanker *Tamano* struck a buoy and ran up on a ledge near Hussey Shoal in Portland, Maine. The large tanker spilled 100,000 gallons of heavy petroleum into the waters of Portland harbor and a containment boom was secured around the grounded vessel. *Photo by Portland Press Herald courtesy Guy Gannett Publishing.* **Below:** Days later, still hard aground and the oil slick is shown in the foreground as a small coastal tanker unloads cargo from the grounded tanker. *Photo courtesy United States Coast Guard.*

New York City fire department boats together with Coast Guard units worked into the early morning hours of June 2, 1973, to extinguish the blaze which left the *C.V. Sea Witch,* above, and the *Esso Brussels,* below, smouldering hulks. While outbound from New York the *Sea Witch* lost steering control and rammed the tanker as she lay at anchor with a full load of crude oil aboard. The fire that followed took 16 lives and turned the two vessels into piles of blackened steel. *Photos courtesy of the United States Coast Guard.*

Above: On December 18, 1973, the Greek tanker *Armonia* grounded on the riprap in the Cape Cod Canal at Bournedale. Tricky currents were the cause of the accident, and the ship suffered a gash in her bow below the waterline but was in no danger and able to continue her trip when pulled off the rocks by the tugs. The grounding closed the canal for four hours. *Photo by William P. Quinn.* **Below:** In Cape Cod Bay, a towing hawser broke and the Bouchard Oil Barge *B No. 105* went aground on Sandy Neck Beach in Barnstable, Massachusetts on February 5, 1974. A Coast Guard helicopter was used to haul out the hawser so that the tug could pull the barge off the beach the next day. The *B No. 105* appears later on page 206. *Photo by Gordon Caldwell, Hyannis, Massachusetts.*

The Cypriot tanker *Athenian Star* anchored off Portsmouth, N.H. in February 1975, after sustaining sea damage on a trip across the Atlantic. The ship had underwater cracks in her hull as well as a waterline hole in her port bow where steel plates had been torn off in heavy seas. Her cargo was discharged into coastal tankers while at anchor and then she proceeded to Boston for repairs. *United States Coast Guard photos by Bill Van Valkenburg and Richard Griggs.*

Above: The Liberian tanker *Spartan Lady* broke up in heavy seas 150 miles south of Martha's Vineyard Island on April 4, 1975. The crew gathered on the after part of the stern as Coast Guard helicopters arrived to rescue them. **Below:** Days later the Coast Guard used gunfire to sink the bow section of the ill-fated *Spartan Lady*. The cargo of 500,000 gallons of oil was lost. *Photos courtesy of the United States Coast Guard, New York, N.Y.*

This photograph was made from one of the rescue helicopters hovering above the after deck of the *Spartan Lady* just as the basket reaches the deck. The lift was hazardous with winds at 50 knots and visibility on scene was less than a mile with heavy driving snow. *Photo courtesy of the United States Coast Guard, New York, N.Y.*

195

The survivors of the *Spartan Lady* were landed by Coast Guard helicopters at Barnstable Airport on Cape Cod. One man was lost to heart failure during the flight in from the scene. One man fell to his knees to thank the Almighty for his rescue. The others were very happy to reach dry land. *Photo by Lou LaPrade.*

The Federal Government issued new edicts on February 1, 1977 to tighten up marine safety rules and practices to prevent future oil spills. A new safety board was set up to review the regulations and to develop new procedures. A department head said that the frequency of tanker accidents in domestic waters was intolerable. New regulations for navigational equipment and communications, and better standards for equipment and personnel on vessels steaming in United States waters were implemented. The main problem was a larger population using more oil than the country could produce. Greater reliance on imported oil was the result, bringing more tankers and more accidents. The majority of the tankers arriving at United States ports are of foreign registry. Most oil is transported in the "flags of convenience" group. These ships are registered in Liberia, Panama, or Honduras and have lower safety standards than do the major shipping nations. Such standards countenance poorer ship construction and maintenance, less experienced crews, and officers who could not pass the rigid United States maritime tests of competence. The main reason for this is economics. If the oil were transported in American tankers the cost would be three times greater than in the foreign ships. Legislation was introduced in the United States Congress to require foreign ships to adhere to our regulations when entering American ports but was not enacted.

Above: On December 15, 1976, the Liberian tanker *Argo Merchant* grounded on the shoals 29 miles southeast of Nantucket Island. The next day, the Coast Guard Cutter *Vigilant* was on the scene to take command of salvage operations. *Photo by William P. Quinn.* **Below:** An HH-3F helicopter ferrying the Coast Guard Atlantic Strike Force Team hovers over the bow of the *Argo Merchant* as the men continued to battle to save the ship. *Photo courtesy of the United States Coast Guard.*

On December 17, 1976, two days after the *Argo Merchant* grounding, the *SS Sansenina* exploded at an oil terminal at San Pedro, California. Eight persons died and about 50 were injured. Unloading of the vessel's crude oil cargo had been completed and ballasting was in progress when a flash flame started aft of the midship house near the cargo manifold and carried into the No. 10 tanks. Smoke at right is from the bridge house and from a large section of the deck which fell into the terminal yard. *Photo courtesy of the United States Coast Guard, Washington, D.C.*

On December 15, 1976, the Liberian tanker *Argo Merchant* went aground on the Nantucket Shoals, 29 miles southeast of Nantucket Island. The vessel was 18 miles off course. The Coast Guard launched a massive effort to unload the ship, but Mother Nature beat them to it. Six days later, in stormy weather, she split in two, spilling 7½ million gallons of bunker oil into the Atlantic near one of the most famous tourist beach areas in the United States, Cape Cod, and adjacent to one of the richest fishing grounds in the world, Georges Bank. In 1967, while the *Torrey Canyon* disaster had precipitated a total media effort, the *Argo Merchant*, in 1976, turned out a media blitzkrieg. The accident presaged a series of ship disasters that seemed to escalate out of all proportion.

On December 17th two days after the *Argo Merchant* grounded, the Liberian tanker *Sansinena* exploded in Long Beach, California, killing eight persons and injuring fifty. On December 27th, the Liberian tanker *Olympic Games* grounded off New Jersey, spilling 135,500 gallons of oil. On December 30th, the Panamanian tanker *Grand Zenith,* with a 38 man crew and 8 million gallons of oil, was long overdue at Fall River, Massachusetts. Eight days later two life jackets from the ship were recovered 240 miles south of Halifax, Nova Scotia. On January 10, 1977, the coastal tanker *Chester A. Poling* broke up off Cape Ann, Massachusetts, in stormy seas with the loss of one man. The tanker was fortunately empty at the time. On January 28, 1977, the Bouchard barge *B. No 65* ran aground in Buzzards Bay, Massachusetts, off Wings Neck and spilled about 100,000 gallons of fuel oil. On February 4, 1977, the barge *Ethel H.* ran aground in the Hudson River near Bear Mountain and spilled 420,000 gallons of oil.

Above: The angry Atlantic whips up the white water around the grounded *Argo Merchant*. The weather out on the shoals in December is never good, only bad or worse. After two days aground the ship began to creak and groan. *Photo courtesy of the United States Coast Guard.* **Below:** After returning from the wreck scene Captain Lynn Hein (left) and Lt. Cmdr. Barry Chambers held a press conference at Otis base to describe conditions at the wreck for the media. Chambers was Commander of the Atlantic Strike Force Team. *Photo by Gordon Caldwell, Hyannis, Massachusetts.*

Above: On board an HH-3F Coast Guard helicopter over the *Argo Merchant,* a battery of news photographers, including the Author, (with earphones) prepare to make television news film of the grounded tanker. *Photo by Jack Cryan, Jr.* **Below:** On December 19th, the oil leaking from the ship blackened the after decks as the slick on top of the water spread out for miles down wind. *Ektachrome by William P. Quinn.*

Above: Rough weather split the tanker in half and she continued to emit heavy blobs of oil three days later. The strong currents on the shoals moved the bow section away from the heavier stern section. In the air, the scene had a tragic beauty in this view from a Coast Guard flying boat. *Photo by Jack Cryan, Jr.* **Below:** On December 24th the wreck was still leaking oil. The slick spread out for almost one hundred miles. *Ektachrome by William P. Quinn.*

Above: The oil barge Bouchard *B No. 65,* carrying 3.3 million gallons of home heating oil, ran aground off Wings Neck in Buzzards Bay on the night of January 28, 1977. The cargo tanks were holed and leaking. Another barge was brought alongside to unload the cargo from the damaged *B No. 65.* **Below:** While tugs maneuver and break ice, the oil spill contractor arrives to clean up the mess. *Photos by William P. Quinn.*

Above: Wings Neck, which is normally deserted in the winter became a beehive of activity as oil spill specialists work on the ice to clean up from the grounded barge. **Below:** Some oil patches drifted around in Buzzards Bay. To avoid further pollution the Coast Guard attempted to burn the oil with a wicking agent atop the ice. About 2,000 gallons of oil were burned but the resulting air pollution was worse than the oil on the ice. *Aerial photos by William P. Quinn.*

A major oil spill on the Hudson River occurred early in February, 1977, when the barge *Ethel H.* struck Con Hook Rock, near West Point, resulting in the loss of 420,000 gallons of No. 6 industrial oil. Coast Guard oil strike teams were brought to the scene for the cleanup. In the photograph above, a derrick is holding up the listing barge to allow pumps to transfer the oil to another vessel. *Photo courtesy of the United States Coast Guard, Washington, D.C.*

Above: The coastal tanker *Vincent Tibbetts* went aground on the rocks at Cow Island just outside Portland, Maine, on August 3, 1977. The vessel was carrying 2,900 barrels of oil at the time. She was pulled off the rocks the next day, without damage, by the tug *Celtic*. There was no oil spill in the incident. *Photo courtesy of Guy Gannett Publications, Portland, Maine.* **Below:** A severe storm with 60 m.p.h. winds whipped through southern New England and the 712' American tanker *Achilles* ran aground in Narragansett Bay near the Mount Hope bridge on January 9, 1978. The ship had a cargo of more than twelve million gallons of home heating oil on board, but she was stranded in mud and did not punch any holes in her hull. The next morning with a battery of tugboats pushing, the vessel was freed and escorted to her unloading docks. *Aerial photo by William P. Quinn.*

205

The ultimate hogging of a vessel occurred on January 31, 1978, in Newington, New Hampshire, when the Bouchard oil barge *B No. 105* (page 192) was loading a million gallons of No. 6 heavy industrial oil. The forward and after tanks were loaded first and the hull could not stand the stress and split like an eggshell. About 7,000 gallons of oil were spilled into the Piscatacqua River above Portsmouth, N.H., and had to be cleaned up. The barge was towed to New Jersey for repairs. *Wide World Photos.*

The great blizzard of February 7, 1978, caused some marine mishaps in the Boston area. Above, the 682' Greek oil tanker *Global Hope* went aground near Bakers Island just outside Salem harbor during the height of the storm. The 47' pilot boat *Can Do,* answering the SOS out of Salem Harbor, was lost with a crew of five. The ship was in no immediate danger on the shoals. About 15,000 gallons of oil spilled out of the cracked hull and floated off with the tide. The oil ultimately washed up on Cape Cod bay beaches in Wellfleet. The ship was refloated a month later and towed into Boston for repairs. *Aerial photo by William P. Quinn.*

On February 7, 1978, New England was buried under a blizzard. Twenty-seven inches of snow fell in Boston. It was one of the worst storms in history. During the worst part of the storm the Greek tanker *Global Hope* went aground outside Salem harbor, spilling about 15,000 gallons of oil. In March, another supertanker ran aground off the coast of France near Brittany. The *Amoco Cadiz* lost her steering in the English Channel and grounded off Portsall. The huge tanker split in half and out gushed 68 million gallons of crude oil that spread along the beaches and wiped out the entire marine fisheries industry there. Formerly, fish, lobsters, shellfish - especially the oysters - and seaweed were all harvested in abundance off the northern coast of the Breton Peninsula. Thousands of volunteers from all over Europe came to France to help clean up the mess. In January, 1979, a navigation error caused the 630' tanker *Afghanistan* to go aground about 10 miles east of Nantucket Island. The vessel was carrying almost ten million gallons of gasoline and was very close to the site of the *Argo Merchant* disaster of 1976. The ship was grounded for about two hours, and then, at high tide, she backed off into deep water. She then continued her voyage to Boston. There was no damage to the hull, nor was any oil spilled. Just a case of a wrong turn.

In 1969, the General Dynamics Corporation had proposed to build a fleet of nuclear-powered submarine tankers. The incentive for the proposal was the oil discovery at Prudhoe Bay in Alaska. The company reasoned that this would be the safest and most economical way to move oil to the east coast of the United States, an area of the greatest need. The submarines would be immune to the hazards of fog and storms and could travel under the ice field. Technical feasibility and cost evaluation showed the plan to be highly practical. Many experts described the plan as dangerous and impractical.

The stern section of the British tanker *Kurdistan* lies awash about 45 miles northeast of Nova Scotia. The ship broke in half on March 15, 1979, spilling about a third of her 29,662 tons of heavy bunker oil. The tanker was believed to have struck a growler, a submerged iceberg while steaming through Cabot Strait on her way to Quebec, Canada. *Wide World Photos.*

CHAPTER TWELVE

In 1970, the United States Coast Guard opened up their new air station at Otis Air Base in Falmouth on Cape Cod. The new base replaced two older stations at Salem, Massachusetts on the north shore and Quonset Point in Rhode Island to combine operations at a central point for the First Coast Guard District. On March 4, 1971, a Greek freighter rammed the Newport, Rhode Island, bridge. The Navy and Coast Guard battled high winds to free the *MV George Pan.* The 200-foot vessel had hit one of the two main towers supporting the bridge across Narragansett Bay and had a hole torn in its side. In August, 1971, the United States abandoned its traditional position on the three mile limit in her territorial waters in favor of the twelve mile limit.

In July, 1972, three oil rig supply ships hooked on to a half-million ton iceberg and towed it a quarter of a mile. The incident occurred off the coast of Labrador when the iceberg began bearing down on the oil drilling rig, *Typhoon.* The supply vessels, hooked together with a wire rope, girdled the iceberg and towed it clear of the drilling rig. In April, 1973, the Coast Guard announced that it was discontinuing three Atlantic weather patrol stations. The posts to be terminated were: Bravo, Charley and Delta. They were in the mid-Atlantic and were maintained by 225-foot cutters. The ships provided weather and navigational data, and were available for "search and rescue" missions in the area of the stations. The Coast Guard said that modern technology in the "jet age," with navigation and communications by satellite, had now negated the need for these patrols far out at sea.

On May 16, 1975, the tug *William C. Gaynor* was pulling a barge east in Rockaway Inlet just south of Coney Island, New York. The sea was calm, and suddenly the tug turned over and sank in twelve feet of water. Four crewmen who were on deck were tossed into the bay and were saved by passing vessels. Four other men were trapped inside the overturned hull. Coast Guard helicopters and rescue boats were on the scene quickly but it took two hours to get the men to the surface. The men were in the bunkroom and had an air bubble to keep them alive. New York City Police scuba divers swam inside the hull and led the men out, swimming to the surface. In 1976, the Coast Guard set up guidelines to assist groups in monitoring Citizens Band radio frequencies in order to relay boating distress information to Coast Guard "search and rescue" operations. Most boatmen depend on the UHF-FM marine radio. The Coast Guard always montiors channel 16, (156.8 MHz) which is the international distress and calling frequency. However, since many small boats carry only the CB radio, special groups monitor these frequencies in order to protect the boating public.

In 1976, the United States celebrated its Bicentennial Year with festivals and parades. The celebration began when President Ford visited Concord, Massachusetts—where it all began, 200 years ago in April 1776. On July 4th, Operation Sail was held in New York City, where a gathering of tall sailing ships from all over the world was viewed by six million people. In May, 1977 the Coast Guard announced that the century old system of storm warnings was to be supplanted by modern technology. The use of red flags known as "Maggie's Drawers" was to be replaced by a series of short wave radio broadcasts on the Atlantic Coast from Connecticut down to Delaware. Loud complaints from the boating public reversed the decision and the flags still wave, warning boaters of approaching weather. An amusing story came from London when the advertising agency for a well known vodka dreamed up a unique ad. It showed a young woman, floating in the ocean; her life jacket had the word "Titanic" printed on it, and she had a drink in her hand. The caption said: "Well, they said anything could happen." After a barrage of complaints the ad was withdrawn, and a substitute was used.

The fishing vessel *Alton A.* and a Coast Guard 44-foot motor lifeboat were smashed onto the rocks at Cape Elizabeth, Maine, on December 5, 1972. The fishing boat had gone aground, and the Coast Guard boat went to the aid of the grounded vessel when seas became worse and both boats were in trouble. The crews of both were assisted ashore by hawsers, hand over hand through the waves with help from shore. Efforts to save the boats were carried on through the night hours but were futile. Later the 44-footer was hauled closer to shore by a bulldozer and lifted off with a crane. The fishing boat was lost. *Photos courtesy of the Maine Historical Society, Portland, Maine.*

Above: On May 12, 1974 the Canadian freighter *Jennifer* was on her way from St. John, N.B. to New York City with a cargo of 1,300 tons of raw sugar. While off the coast of Maine the cargo shifted, resulting in a 14 degree list. The Coast Guard escorted the vessel into Bar Harbor and grounded her on the shore near the Yarmouth ferry terminal. **Below:** The wet sticky cargo was unloaded onto the Bar Harbor municipal pier from where it was trucked away. The *Jennifer* then left for repairs at a shipyard in East Boston. The ship was lost on December 2, 1974, when she sank in Lake Michigan during a gale, twenty miles northeast of Milwaukee, Wisconsin. The 15 crewmen were saved. *Photos by John Megas, Ellsworth American, Ellsworth, Maine.*

Above: The Soviet research vessel *Belogorsk* ran up on a stone jetty in Woods Hole harbor on Cape Cod, September 3, 1974. The ship was in the United States to take part in a cooperative fisheries research program. She was assisted off the rocks without damage by the Coast Guard tug *Towline* and she tied up at the Woods Hole Institute pier. **Below:** The 65-foot tugboat *Matey One* went aground at the entrance to Westport, Massachusetts harbor early in the morning on November 13, 1974. The tug had been engaged in salvage work when rising winds forced them to head for safe harbor. The crew of four were saved, but the vessel was a total loss. *Photos by William P. Quinn.*

Above: The 10-meter sloop *Trull* was fighting heavy seas in Cape Cod Bay on the night of October 27, 1974. Her anchors dragged and she went aground on Sandy Neck in Barnstable. The Coast Guard removed the crew by helicopter and the pretty sloop lay helpless on her side at low tide the next day while many Cape Codders drove down to view the wreck. *Photo by P.T. Wolf, courtesy of the Yarmouth Register.* **Below:** A marked contrast on the next day as most of her usable parts had been stripped and looted. All that was left was a smashed hull and broken dreams of her owner. *Photo by Gordon C. Caldwell, Hyannis, Massachusetts.*

The New Bedford fishing vessel *Algarve II* lost her bearings in a storm on the night of November 25, 1974, and piled up on the rock jetty at the entrance to Nantucket Harbor. The three man crew was rescued by Coast Guard Helicopter. The vessel was a total loss. **Above:** Later the stranded hull was used to depict a helicopter rescue for a local film production about Coast Guard operations around Cape Cod. *Photo by Chief Charles Moore, U.S.C.G.* **Below:** About 4 a.m. on February 28, 1975, a fire swept a 126-foot ex-Navy minesweeper named the *Arctic Fox* moored at the old Hingham shipyard near Boston, Massachusetts. For the next ten hours Coast Guard vessels worked with at least seven fire departments trying to put out the blaze. Finally at 2 p.m. that afternoon, the *Arctic Fox* was scuttled at the pier in order to put out the fire. *Photo courtesy of the United States Coast Guard.*

The Japanese freighter *Musashino Maru* went aground at Searsport, Maine, early in the morning of February 2, 1976. There was a heavy rain squall, and visibility was at a minimum. Her bottom was holed by the rocks and the ship was high and dry at low tide. For twelve days the freighter was an attraction as she lay near the shore. Residents of the area had to hire guards to protect their property. *Photo by Steve Lang, Owls Head, Maine.*

On the 15th of February the Eastern Canada Towing Co., Ltd. pulled her off and towed her to Boston for repairs. Damage was minimal and the ship went back into service. *Photo by John Laitin of the Republican Journal, Belfast, Maine.*

Above: The cement barge *Angela* was wrecked on the Hens and Chickens, south of Westport, Massachusetts, on March 4, 1971. The barge was at anchor when a squall caused her to swing around and drag onto the ledge. Leaks solidified the cement cargo and the vessel became a total loss. Five years later on May 5, 1976, the barge *Centennial II* went aground at the same spot during a storm. The container barge had a three million dollar cargo of French wines, liquor, furniture and automobile radial tires. The crew of the McAlister Bros. Co. barge was removed, and the next day a crew of salvors from Falmouth - the A. & R. Marine Salvage Corporation - boarded the barge by helicopter and began salvage of the cargo. A few days later, in court, attorneys argued ownership and salvage rights. On May 20th, the barge broke up and sank in high winds before all of the cargo had been removed. **Below:** Tragedy struck the Provincetown fishing fleet on October 24, 1976, when the 64-foot scalloper *Patricia Marie* sank three miles east of Eastham on Cape Cod, Massachusetts. Seven men were lost. Cause of the sinking was thought to be swamping, when the cargo of several thousand pounds of scallops shifted and rolled the vessel over. A few days later, divers working from the deck of the Coast Guard cutter *Bittersweet* located the hull and went down in search of the bodies of the crewmen but none was found. *Aerial photos by William P. Quinn.*

Above: On October 30, 1976, Boston firefighters were called to Commonwealth Pier to battle a cargo fire aboard the Italian freighter *Pia Costa.* Thirty-six tons of rags, leather and plastics were afire and burned for four hours before being controlled. **Below:** The ship took on a twenty degree list from the weight of the water used to fight the fire. The list was corrected by a shift in ballast. About $60,000 in damage was caused by the blaze. None of the crew was injured. *Photos by Stanley Forman.*

The New Bedford fishing vessel *Sylvester F. Whalen* came ashore on Cisco beach on Nantucket on November 4, 1976. The 91' vessel was returning from the Georges Bank and had developed a bad leak. Electrical power was lost and when pumps could not keep her afloat the Captain decided to beach his vessel. The Coast Guard removed the crew of six by helicopter. The vessel was a total loss. *Photo by Jeff Barnard, Nantucket, Mass.*

The winter of 1977 was a cold one. Northerly winds built up the ice three miles outside Nantucket harbor. Pressure ridges were three feet thick in some places. The motor ferry *Uncatena*, assisted by the Coast Guard cutter *Yankton*, spent 2½ hours pushing, backing, and breaking ice to get into port to bring in the much needed supplies to the island. The ferry suffered minor hull damage while breaking ice. The regular ferry run from Woods Hole normally takes three hours. This trip took over five hours. *Aerial photo by William P. Quinn, plane piloted by Brian Kelly.*

Above: The British trawler *Croesus* ran aground off Tuckernuck Island near Nantucket on January 16, 1977. The vessel from Hull, England, was being delivered to Nova Scotia when she went off course and got lost in a blinding snow storm. The Coast Guard removed the crew of three by lifeboat from the Brant Point Station on Nantucket. The trawler lay on the shoal all winter and was badly damaged by ice floes. The 78-foot hull was a total loss. *Photo by William P. Quinn, plane piloted by Brian Kelly.* **Below:** Picked up just before they got their feet wet, two South Portland Maine lobstermen climb aboard a Coast Guard patrol boat after their boat went down on October 14, 1977 in Portland, Maine harbor. The low tide caused the vessel to ride onto an old submerged piling, roll over and sink. *Photo by Jim Daniels, courtesy Portland Press Herald.*

Above: A mishap resulting from the Great Blizzard of February 7, 1978, was the *Peter Stuyvesant,* a former Hudson River Day Line steamer. The ship had served as an annex to Anthony's Pier 4 Restaurant in Boston and had been a popular watering spot. During the storm an extra high tide floated the vessel off concrete pilings and tossed her into the harbor where she sank. A valuable collection of ship models was lost in the accident.*Photo by William P. Quinn.* **Below:** On December 2, 1978, the fishing vessel *United States* developed a leak, filled and sank. The crew managed to escape in a dory and then spent four hours bobbing around on ten-foot swells. They were picked up by the Coast Guard cutter *Decisive* about thirty miles south of Newport, Rhode Island. They were spotted by an HU-16 flying boat from the Coast Guard Air Station on Cape Cod. *Photo by the United States Coast Guard.*

Above: The last of the sidewheel steamboats from the Hudson River came near to being enshrined as a museum but nature played a trump card. The steamer *Alexander Hamilton* grounded on a sandbar near shore at Atlantic Highlands, New Jersey, and falling into disrepair, seemingly destined to rot away. On September 15, 1977, in an effort to save the historic vessel, she was hauled off the bar and towed to the Navy pier at Earle, New Jersey for temporary berthing before starting a journey up the Hudson River for restoration. *Photo by William P. Quinn.* **Below:** On November 8, 1978, a violent storm caught the veteran ship in an exposed position and damaged her almost beyond repair. She sank in 16 feet of water. Restoration may take a little longer. . . .*Aerial photograph by Francis J. Duffy, Pilot-Lt. Hugh O'Doherty, United States Coast Guard.*

In mid December, 1978, the United States Coast Guard came upon an unidentified fishing vessel off Cape Cod flying no flag, and without name or number on the hull. A routine search of the fish holds turned up about 33 tons of marijuana. The vessel was brought to the Coast Guard base in Boston, Massachusetts and the eleven crewmen aboard were arrested.

The prevention of smuggling has always been one of the functions of the United States Coast Guard since its founding in 1790 as the Revenue Marine. In the 1920's the Coast Guard again had to wage war on smuggling as the rumrunners ran wild during the fourteen years of prohibition. Now, in the 1970's, some of the lessons learned in the rum war are being recalled as the Coast Guard is again battling smugglers. This time the contraband is marijuana. The cargo is different, but the pattern is the same - a fast boat, illicit cargo, and a supply ship off shore outside the twelve mile limit. A boat load of whiskey was once worth a few thousand dollars to the rumrunner that could land it successfully. A boat load of "pot" is worth up to a million dollars to the criminals. The smugglers try new and different ways to bring it into the country.

Expensive luxury yachts, some costing one hundred thousand dollars or more, are being used in this illegal trade. Some have been caught and confiscated, with tons of the weed on board. There are many secluded coves and inlets on the New England coastline where a yacht could hide. Even if detected by local residents, it might not be suspected because of its aura of opulent respectability. The Coast Guardsmen have arrested many persons who were suspected of smuggling and have seized numerous yachts and boats; but, as with the liquor war, for every one caught, four or five more escape.

On December 20, 1978, the *Mostefa Ben Boulaid* arrived in Boston harbor from Algeria with 31 million gallons of liquid natural gas. Elaborate precautions were set up by the Coast Guard to prevent any accidents during her passage through the harbor to the gas terminal in Everett, Massachusetts. The huge ship seemed almost as large as the Boston skyscrapers.

In 1978, concern was voiced toward the importation of liquid natural gas and its storage in terminals in densely populated areas. The product is extremely hazardous, and a major disaster in a city could well kill a hundred thousand people. The gas is cooled to minus 259 degrees F at which point it turns into a liquid. The gas in the liquid state is highly condensed and can be carried economically in especially built tankers. The L.N.G. vessels operate quite differently from conventional tankers. There are no inexperienced crewmen. Each man is highly trained for his job, and these operations are costly. L.N.G. tankers are the most expensive merchant ships that are built.

The Coast Guard bears the responsibility for the safety of all commercial vessels in United States waters. They guard against accidents, sabotage, and vandalism. The Coast Guard has set up special standards for L.N.G. tanker movements. The liquid gas is hazardous, but is not the most dangerous cargo handled. There are periodic arrivals in Boston, Massachusetts of L.N.G. tankers. These vessels have to submit to operating restrictions inside the harbor. The Coast Guard sets up a moving security zone around these vessels while they move in the channel. In Boston, no other ship traffic is permitted, and airline landings and takeoffs from Logan Airport are prohibited in the area surrounding these ships while they are entering the harbor. The tankers are escorted into the unloading pier. No night operations are allowed. The safeguards built into the L.N.G. operations have thus far been successful in preventing accidents.

On February 18, 1979, four airmen aboard a Coast Guard HH-3F helicopter were killed when their aircraft crashed into the Atlantic Ocean. The helicopter was on a rescue mission 180 miles southeast of Cape Cod in thick weather. The sea was rough and, at the time of the accident, the aircraft was hovering over a fishing vessel to remove an injured crewman. A huge wave struck the nose of the aircraft on the right side and it rolled into the sea. One airman from the helicopter survived. A photograph of the aircraft appears on page 197. *Photo courtesy of the United States Coast Guard.*

The past 100 years have seen many changes in ships and shipwrecks around the New England coastline. The disasters in the late nineteenth century were no less spectacular, but everything seemed to move at a slower pace in those days. The storms were just as bad, but the sailing ships looked prettier, even when they were wrecked - and they didn't pollute. Sail gave way to steam, with its power and reliability for schedule. However, the ships continued to be involved in accidents along the coast as man, in spite of his innate intelligence, can still make mistakes. The wireless-radio helped to save many lives on the high seas; and improvements in modern technology enabled mariners to steer a truer course.

The Life Savers acquired better equipment to help save the imperiled sailors. The motor lifeboat relieved surfmen from the toil of rowing, and the helicopter has supplanted the line throwing gun and the breeches buoy. The numerous aids to navigation - radio, loran and depth finders have helped to bring the ships home safely. A shipwreck is a comparatively rare occurrence today - in this age of automation and computers. The development of ships has reduced the accidents. Today a few large highly automated vessels do the work of many small ones. The design, power, reliability and developments in navigational devices result in fewer ships experiencing wrecks. The New England weather is still the same - damnable and ornery. Storms rage along the coast, but the sailor knows that they are approaching long before they arrive, and he can batten down and double up the lines and watch the storm go by while he lies in a safe harbor.

The End

EPILOGUE

There is ample evidence today of the numerous shipwrecks that have occurred around New England. The remains of steamers, sailing ships and barges dot the entire coastline, vessels that were run aground beyond salvage, stark reminders of the past days of navigation by dead reckoning. Divers continue to explore sunken ships in water too deep to record on film. Samuel Johnson said: "All history, so far as it is not supported by contemporary evidence, is romance." Older seafaring men spin the nostalgic yarns about their days before the mast and captivate those who come after with vivid tales of disasters and rescue. Some of the strandings and subsequent re-floating of vessels along New England's shorelines have been examined in this book. The ocean bottom off-shore is littered with hundreds more, sunken hulls - each with an epic tale of disaster.

Contributing most to the long maritime annals of New England were the sailing ships. Theirs was one of the most fascinating periods in history. The beauty of sailing along under acres of canvas was magnificent, but the days of sail have dwindled to a few special occasions. The era of steam came and the coal burners gave way to oil. The diesel engine challenged the steamship and, atomic power, while it has been improved, has not been very popular. The oil gets more expensive and less available each day. The return to coal however, seems unlikely. There is a proposal to build a new and modern sailing ship. An automated vessel that will retire the steamers and give birth to a new era on the sea. The results should be interesting. History usually repeats itself because it has so few readers - and the wind is free. That is the way of ships.

On February 8, 1979, a large waterfront fire at the Bush Terminal Pier in Brooklyn. The Coast Guard cutter *Mahoning* along with New York harbor tugs, police and fire boats fought the blaze along with thirty-five land based fire companies. It took two and a half hours to bring the blaze under control. *Photo courtesy of the United States Coast Guard, Washington, D.C.*

On June 18, 1979, the tanker *Exxon Chester* rammed the Liberian freighter *Regal Sword* in dense fog about 30 miles southeast of Chatham, off Cape Cod, Massachusetts. The freighter sank in the Atlantic and her crew of 38 cleared in a lifeboat just as she went down. They were all picked up by the tanker and taken to Boston. On arrival in the Hub, crewmembers of the *Regal Sword* said that the two lookouts on the bridge were both below having supper at the time of the accident. The tanker *Exxon Chester* is shown as she arrived in Boston on the 19th with a smashed bow.

ACKNOWLEDGMENTS

The search for photographs in this book extended all over the United States. There were contributions from many different private collections. Some were borrowed and copied while many others were purchased. I found one in a flea market and another in an antique auction. A grateful "Thank You" is extended to all those who loaned or gave me photographs and others who aided me in the search for information. There are many others, whose names appear in the credit lines under each photograph and I wish to thank one and all. In any work of this magnitude there are those special people who have worked with me to bring the book to its final stage: Paul Morris, Charlie Sayle, Jim and Alice Wilson, Bob Beattie, Bill Fuller, Jr., Captain W.J.L. Parker, U.S.C.G. (Ret.), John Lochhead, Gordon Caldwell, Gardner Roberts, Laura Brown, Frank Claes, David Crockett, Roger Dunkerley, Babs Eason, Carolyn Ritger, Mr. & Mrs. E.K. Haviland, Peter Eisele, Prof. Robert H. Farson, Captain Biff Bowker, Arline Gilman, Marnee Small, Ed Lohr, Capt. Thomas F. Currie, Herb Williams, Ralph L. Snow, Barry Eager, Chad Smith, Armand Guarino and John Ullman. Again, deep gratitude to all those who helped me in the acquisition and assembly of this material.

W.P.Q.

The *Flagstaff*, a high speed hydrofoil vessel was transferred to the Coast Guard from the United States Navy in 1976, in order for the service to carry out an evaluation of the cutter. Some of the "search and rescue" and law enforcement missions of the Coast Guard require high speed and the evaluation was to determine the performance of the hydrofoil in this type of mission in an actual operational environment. The ship was sent to Boston, Massachusetts for commissioning. The *Flagstaff* arrived at Woods Hole in July of 1977. The vessel operated for 14 months and during that time there were numerous problems with the turbine as well as other mechanical difficulties so that in September, 1978, the cutter was decommissioned. *Photo courtesy of the United States Coast Guard.*

BIBLIOGRAPHY

American Sailing Coasters of the North Atlantic,
    Paul C. Morris

Commonwealth, Giantess of the Sound,
    Roger Williams McAdam

Compact History of the United States Coast Guard,
    Howard V. L. Bloomfield

Fire Aboard, Frank Rushbrook

Four Masted Schooners of the East Coast,
    Paul C. Morris

Life Saving Nantucket, Edouard A. Stackpole

Old Nantasket, Dr. William M. Bergan

Nightboat, George W. Hilton

Penobscot Bay Steamboat Album, Allie Ryan

Rum War at Sea, Malcolm F. Willoughby

Salts of the Sound, Roger Williams McAdam

Ship Ashore!, Jeannette Edwards Rattray

Steamboat Lore of the Penobscot, John M. Richardson

Storms and Shipwrecks of New England,
    Edward Rowe Snow

The Down Easters, Basil Lubbock

The Great Coal Schooners of New England,
    Capt. W. J. L. Parker

The Great Liners, (The Seafarers)
    Time-Life Books, Melvin Maddocks

The Island Steamers,
    Paul C. Morris and Joseph F. Morin

The Last Sail Down East, Giles M.S. Todd

The Making of Modern America, Canfield & Wilder

The Perils of the Port of New York,
    Jeannette Edwards Rattray

The Story of America in Pictures, Alan C. Collins

The Target Ship in Cape Cod Bay, Noel W. Beyle

LIBRARIES

Boston Public Library, Boston, Mass.

Eldredge Library, Chatham, Mass.

Falmouth Public Library, Falmouth, Mass.

New Bedford Public Library, New Bedford, Mass.

St. Petersburg Public Library, St. Petersburg, Fla.

Steamship Historical Society of America Library
    at the University of Baltimore, Baltimore, Maryland

GOVERNMENT PUBLICATIONS

United States Coast Pilot 1966 Editions
    (1)   Eastport to Cape Cod,
    (2)   Cape Cod to Sandy Hook

United States Coast Guard Annual Reports,
    1915 to 1920

United States Lighthouse Board Annual Reports,
    1872, 1873, 1876

United States Life Saving Service Annual Reports,
    1876 to 1914

Merchant Vessels of the United States, 1873 to 1976

Proceedings of the Marine Safety Council,
    January 1953 to March-April 1979

PERIODICALS

Down East Magazine

Ships and the Sea Magazine - 1951 to 1959

Smithsonian - February 1978

Steamboat Bill - 1940's to 1970's

Tow Line - Moran Towing & Trans. Co.,
    New York, N.Y.

The World Almanac - 1979.

NEWSPAPERS

Bath Daily Times, Bath, Maine

Boston Herald, Boston Globe, Boston, Mass.

Bridgeport Standard, Bridgeport, Conn.

Cape Codder, Orleans, Mass.

Cape Cod Standard Times, Hyannis, Mass.

New Bedford Mercury, New Bedford Standard Times,
    New Bedford, Mass.

New York Times, New York, N.Y.

Providence Journal, Providence, R.I.

Provincetown Advocate, Provincetown, Mass.

MUSEUMS

Bath Marine Museum, Bath, Maine

Bureau of National Archives, Washington, D.C.

Fall River Marine Museum, Fall River, Mass.

Maine Historical Society, Portland, Maine

Mariners Museum, Newport News, Virginia

Mystic Seaport Museum, Mystic, Conn.

Peabody Museum of Salem, Salem, Mass.

Suffolk Marine Museum, West Sayville, N.Y.